Gospelicious

Surrendering to the Love of a Perfect
Father

Aaron Porter

Gospelicious: Soul Architecture Book 1

Copyright © 2022 by Aaron Porter

All rights reserved.

Contents

Foreward

"Our Father, who art in heaven..."

The Lord's Prayer, which is regularly recited by billions of Christians around the world, has also become part of the modern liturgy of recovery. Even though nearly all Twelve-Step programs lack any formal connection with the Christian faith, the prayer that Jesus taught his disciples is still firmly embedded in their DNA, recited at the end of every meeting. As alcoholics, drug addicts, compulsive gamblers, overeaters, workaholics, sex addicts — strugglers of all kinds, along with their partners and adult children — repeat these words, they are breathing a healing affirmation. "We are the children of an all-knowing parent who loves us perfectly."

It is odd, then, that as soon as the meeting is over, many of us return to our old way of thinking. If we do manage to remember that we are the children of a Heavenly Father, we tend to envision Him as apathetic or angry or demanding rather than the type of father Jesus consistently described, a doting father to whom we are securely attached.

We can approach our Higher Power with the affectionate language of a child.

He is our Abba. Our Daddy.

In this powerful little book, Aaron Porter reminds us of our true identity and systematically unpacks its implications. In very specific ways, Aaron challenges us to abandon our orphan thinking, shed our shame, and start to live as though the gospel is really true.

You're going to love this book.

Nate Larkin

Founder of the Samson Society

Note From the Author:

When I was younger I read a lot and tried to study big thoughts, big words, big ideas. But over the years of trying to teach others, I found out how little any of that helped the people I cared for to see an ACTUAL difference in their lives, a real transformation. Then in my mid-twenties, I discovered what the Gospel meant for me. I grew up being taught that the Gospel was the thing that got people saved and then, even though they didn't say it directly, after you were saved it was kind of up to you. Get better at being disciplined. If you don't, God will at the very least be disappointed with you. The entire book of Galatians speaks to how wrong that is. The gospel is the power of God unto salvation, but it is also the power to live out the rest of our lives and discover real joy and freedom, the joy and freedom that Jesus promised but so few seem to experience. Discipline is good, but discipline without an intact Gospel identity simply leads to religious slavery and bondage to shame and fear.

Since that time, what is written on these pages is what I have leaned on to get through the good times and the hard times in my life. In this last season, I have struggled the most with forgiving myself but even in that process, I have gone back time and time again to these thoughts. I have not always loved myself well but I don't know what I would have done if I didn't believe that my Daddy still loved me. It is that love that brings me back home.

I want to take a moment to say what this book is not intended to be. It is not meant to be a book proving anything, defending anything, or impressive to anyone. If you find yourself categorizing what is written within these pages as a penal substitution view, recapitulation, or moral influence view, sigh, then you will be missing the point. This is not a book that will do any kind of a thorough job of being an apologetic book for any particular atonement view. These are things that I needed to understand to root my identity in Christ. They were formed by the church I grew up in, both in regard to pieces I held and others that I threw away. They were formed by people I trusted over my life who helped to flesh out ideas. And they were formed by various books I read that made me ask questions I hadn't before. Ultimately, these are devotional thoughts and are meant to be simple and concise. They are also incomplete and in many ways inaccurate. Don't ask me how they are inaccurate, if I knew that I wouldn't have written them as I did. I would have written them...accurately.

This book is also solely focused on your Gospel identity. How do you see yourself and what stories led you to those beliefs? It begs the question, am I allowing God's view of me through the person and work of Christ to shape how I see myself? Many other aspects of the Christian touch on Gospel transformation and Gospel power. Aspects that concern God's heart for justice for those in need, His hand in the world and countries around us, and the ways that the peace of God has been given to His creation through the person and work of Jesus. All of those things are worthy of our time and our attention. Gospelicious is not addressing those. The three books of Soul Architecture are meant for you to learn how to practically and cleanly understand and address the accusations of your flesh and to find yourself securely moored to a Gospel that is powerful enough, where Jesus is enough, to hold you fast to Your Daddy's love and your status as His beloved child.

My constant hope is that you will find hope that transforms how you see yourself and the world around you. Right now, today, you are who you are, and you are loved. You may be in pain, and there are certainly areas in which you need to grow. If you are serious about growing, you can take a step today. It won't feel like you have changed, because it will only be a step, but growth will come if we keep taking steps. Take more steps forward than you take backward and in five years you will be astounded by your progress. This is your journey and it's so beautiful and precious.

We are all very impatient. It's part of the human condition. We can't help it. But Scripture is full of stories that took decades rather than weeks to unfold. There is no six-week series or 40 days of anything that will create lasting change in you unless you keep moving forward after those 40 days or six weeks have passed. Moses needed 40 years in the wilderness, Paul didn't do any significant ministry for almost a decade after his crazy conversion experience on the road to Damascus. Elijah had to sit for three years after starting his career as a prophet and confronting King Ahab. Years, friend, not one book, not one study, not a perfect sermon or piece of information. Years of life, pain, joy, struggle, and love.

So here we are. I will not try to convince you of anything in this book. I will not try to make you think I have something to offer that is more extraordinary than you, but I will make the case that we are extraordinarily beloved of the coolest Dad ever. Oh how he loves us, and He loves it so much when we engage in this process.

It has been around 20 years since I started writing Soul Architecture, the original book that housed about half of the chapters in Gospelicious. This book, book 1 of the Soul Architecture trilogy will seek to give some clear vocabulary and analogies to try to help us to hold fast to our identities in Christ. With those identities intact we can then, hopefully, accept the love of our perfect Father. Book 2 will seek to address the ways that our flesh seeks to undermine a Gospel narrative in our lives. Finally, book 3 will give practical tools to engage our false narratives and drag them back to the truths here in book 1. That is soul architecture.

I've stopped searching for silver bullets to fix my life or heart because all I ever found was lead. I'm just a normal guy, currently a technical writer for an engineering company. I was a pastor for a long time and I loved that work dearly. I also sometimes wish I could go back and fix so many stupid words I said and things I did. I'm a divorced dad of four kids. No, the divorce is not why I stopped being a pastor, that came later. I have been consistent and honest sometimes, and I have been a moral failure and a hypocrite on many other occasions. I don't have any pedigree that should make you want to continue reading this book if you are looking for deep thoughts or fancy words that you can use to impress a friend over coffee. I'm just a dad, a friend, a part-time screwup, a struggler, a recovering control freak, a griever of huge mistakes, and I'm also a kid that my Daddy adores. Oh man, just writing those words I feel His love, and it brings tears.

My Daddy loves me so much that it overwhelms me, and as the sun is coming up, I need to feel that again. I needed to write it. To see it. To believe it. And to start my day in that loving embrace, whatever the rest of the day may bring.

If that feeling is foreign to you, my heart breaks for you and I WANT it for you.

Introduction:

"So Jesus again said to them, "Truly, truly, I say to you, I am the door of the sheep. All who came before me are thieves and robbers, but the sheep did not listen to them. I am the door. If anyone enters by me, he will be saved and will go in and out and find pasture. The thief comes only to steal and kill and destroy. I came that they may have life and have it abundantly. I am the good shepherd. The good shepherd lays down his life for the sheep." (John 10:7-11)

I wish that I could have seen the look on Jesus' face and heard the tone of His voice when He said those words. Provocative? At the end of those statements, there would be a public debate as to his sanity, whether he was demon-possessed, and His divinity.

I can quickly slide into a kind of life that is no life at all, certainly not the kind of life that Jesus had in mind when He made those declarations. Typically I move into survival mode, a protective state, where I cover myself with my convictions but only at the surface. If anyone were to scratch a little deeper when I am living in such a state, they would find that my beliefs do not always penetrate to the place where they actually affect my life.

How many men and women have learned to live, to truly live? How many have let the deep truths of their miraculous "new creature" identity transform their fears into faith?

These are the examples the Church needs today, saints who are living transformed lives. This life does not come without effort, nor does it come in isolation. We need God's Word, His Spirit, and His Body, all at work in the surrendered life, to experience true inside-out transformation.

There is a certain school of thinkers that believes too much "self-evaluation" is narcissistic and sinful. They might say that we are created to focus attention on our Creator, not sit around thinking about ourselves. It seems like a reasonable argument. However, it is missing a very important component: WE are a part of redemptive history. Who we are in Christ, the new life transformed by the Gospel, is deeply built into the DNA of creation's story and the expression of God's love and personhood. If you take us out of the equation, you take away a beautiful mirror He chose to reflect His character and glory through. We the redeemed are like a tuning fork that, in Christ, resonates the pitch of the glorious mercy and grace of God.

Discovering our life in Christ is worshipful. Such discovery is not self-focused, but absolutely Christ-focused. Do not let anyone rob you of the joy or the journey of discovering your miraculous new creation. You were born to discover who you are within the work of your Sacred Brother. Finding and living that life in Christ is being worshipful in exactly the mode that God ordained.

This is not a pop-psychology-mixed-with-religion book. This is not a health-and-wealth-Gospel book. This is just a, what would it look like to live in the Gospel so truly that it made a practical difference in my odd Western Christian culture book.

Our journey is, unapologetically, a search for our identity in Christ, a Gospel identity. We are looking for freedom and life and a John 15 abiding walk with our Savior. We want to actually encounter that which we have heard about from the pulpit and parish for most of our lives but felt all too little of. We want a reckoned Gospel.

Chapter One

Discovering a Gospel for Christians

I grew up in a great family, in a great little town. My parents loved me well. We attended a small evangelical church where I heard the Bible stories and saw them portrayed on flannel, and I attended a Christian school for the first nine years of my education. Many afternoons, after riding my bike home from school, I would walk along the river behind my house with my dog and my sister's waterproof yellow Sony walkman, Christian music blasting through the headphones.

I was privileged. From my earliest memories, I was given every opportunity to engage my family's faith, and I took that privilege seriously. There was, however, a serpent in my garden.

The church I grew up in was called the Gospel Chapel. So, obviously, it was all about the Gospel. From the beginning, I learned that the Gospel is the power of God unto salvation, and that is for people who are going to hell. The Gospel is the hook we use to pull drowning people from the raging currents of sin. We talked a lot about evangelism and our duty to save people. Once we had pulled sinners to safety, it was their responsibility to become mature.

For us, spiritual maturity consisted of performing certain practices regularly. If you grew up in church you may have been given a list of practices too. This was mine. First, I needed to attend church (at least on Sundays for communion service, Sunday school, morning worship service, and evening service (but God really liked bonus attendance on other days of the week), I needed to have a daily Bible study or devotional time, I needed to pray as much as possible, I needed to not engage in sin, and I needed, of course, to save other people with the Gospel. Oh, and giving money to the church also made the list. I was given a little church-shaped penny bank to take home so that I could bring in my tithe each week, and my parents faithfully taught me how to calculate ten percent of my weekly allowance to put in that little plastic offering box in Sunday school, a representation of my growing maturity.

So, there you have it. Those were my duties. That was what Christianity looked like after you got yourself saved. And what happened if you did not perform all the duties on that list? The consequences could be dire.

I was never explicitly told that God would dislike me or be angry at me if I failed to complete the entire list after I was saved, but I felt it. I felt the shameful sting of God's disapproval every time I stole one of my mom's Victoria's Secret magazines that came in the mail. (I only read them for the articles...) I knew that, in God's eyes, I was a disgusting pervert. If I missed more than a few days of devotions I felt God's disappointment and grew a little more afraid about my future. The only thing keeping me in check was Bible study, I was sure of it. I had hidden His Word in my heart so that I would not sin against Him. That was the point. Just gotta stop sinning.

The worst moments of shame came whenever I had a chance to "witness" to a person and kept my mouth shut because I was scared. I had been told that I might be the ONLY Jesus that other people might ever meet. I might be their only hope. They might go to hell ALL

BECAUSE OF MY COWARDICE. Put this on your list of reasons to distrust me, evidently dozens and dozens of people might have gone to hell because I would not open my little junior-high mouth. What a monster.

When I consider my childhood, I am so grateful for all of the love I received. At the same time, my heart breaks for a boy who wanted to be close to God but was taught that the Gospel is only for those who don't know God yet. Once I had been saved by the Gospel, self-discipline and sin management were my responsibility. Of course, our church would give a tip of the hat to the reality of the indwelling of the Holy Spirit, but the work of the Christian life was clearly up to me. Obedience and discipline had not beet put in their proper place and so they tore at the fabric of the Gospel in my life.

By the time I reached my late teens, that education led me to become a passionate and knowledgeable Pharisee. I moved away from home near the end of my 17th year, got married at 19, and went into full-time vocational ministry the week I turned 20. I did not have a doubt in my head or my heart. I was ready to impact the world for Jesus.

Arrogance is incredibly difficult to see when it is wrapped up in honest passion, conviction, and compassion. Even if both good and bad attributes are present, arrogance will usually be concealed by the better. It is always hard for me to recognize that I am a Pharisee when I'm being applauded for my efforts by groups of people who believe that the Pharisees are the bad guys. It's all very confusing. I must not be a Pharisee or they wouldn't be so stoked about what I am doing.

Hey, dear ones, the Pharisees weren't the bad guys. The Pharisees just had a different way of hiding from their need for Jesus. But Jesus engaged them, taught them, and ate at their houses just like He did the other sinners. I suspect that the reason I used to take such a hard line against Pharisees was the fact that I was more like them than I wanted to believe. Maybe if I said they were bad no one would notice that in my early years of ministry, I was working my ass off to create a few more Pharisees. In those communities, progress consisted of knowing and following the rules and customs/norms of our churchianity. God was a prop in the process far more than He was a participant.

Then, when I was around 23 or 24, I encountered a Gospel that was for me. A Gospel for Christians as well as a Gospel that is the "power of God unto salvation." I learned that my need for the person and work of Jesus is as desperate today and every day as it was before I knew Him at all. I learned that because of who Jesus is and what he did, I am invited into a real relationship with God and that I have been filled with a Spirit that invites me and teaches me how to call Him Daddy.

I have been forever changed by the simplicity of that Gospel. I am sure our church studied Paul's Epistle to the Galatians when I was growing up, so I'm not sure how I managed to miss its main point. Paul was writing to a church of aspiring Pharisees, members of the evangelical industrial complex of its day, and he confronted them with this question: Do you really think you could start this new life by grace and by the Spirit, and then finish it under your own power, a power that was inadequate to begin with? NO! We finish this race under the same power that started it, period. Nothing more.

In the years after my fresh encounter with the Gospel, a few things began to change. I came to begin to recognize the arrogance that was part of my passion and started to escape the bondage of thinking that I had the power to do all of the things I had been obligated to do in childhood. I began to see that a well-intentioned control freak is still a control freak, and whatever I seek to control I will need to manage by the power of my flesh. I started to understand that the duties and attitudes to which I had been indoctrinated and clung to so tightly had produced slavery. My religious faith consisted of bondage. But I also found that obedience and discipline could be a beautiful part of a relationship when love was still fully intact through weak seasons as well as strong ones.

We Americans talk a lot about freedom, but none of us is entirely free. I am not free to do whatever I want in America, land of the free and the home of the brave. There are hundreds of laws that define in great detail what I am not free to do on any given day. And that's a good thing, for if I were to become an anarchist hedonist who did whatever he wanted, with no limits at all, I would simply become a slave to my impulses. Not free.

There is not a soul on earth who does not have a master. Real freedom is a matter of finding the best one.

As I came to understand and engage my identity in Christ, I found myself drawn to my heavenly Father. There, in His loving presence, I found freedom from shame and room to move. My circumstances did not always change (heck, did not usually change). Rather, how I perceived those circumstances and myself within them did change. That is one of the great promises of the Gospel.

God did not promise me a life free of suffering. He told me to expect the exact opposite. The Gospel, however, changes my perspective on my circumstances and in the process changes my reality (more on this later). That is the beauty of the hope and promise that can actually materialize in our lives.

I'm glad that I waited this long to write the last half of this book. In the 20 years since the Gospel found me, I have experienced deep and abiding joy. I have also seen the end of a 25-year marriage and have grieved my part in its failure. I have seen more clearly how my pride has wounded people I thought I was serving. I have seen how my sin and selfishness have wounded people I love. And still, grace abounds.

Even in the ashes, I cannot unsee the completeness of Jesus' person and work, which has made me lovable to my Daddy. In the charred rubble, it shines like a ruby, blinding in its radiance.

I have spent seasons trying to run from my Father's love, but I have yet to escape Him. And even when I am in the pit, His Spirit cries out to Abba, praying the prayer I dare not pray, "Daddy, Love me anyway." And so He does.

Chapter Two

We All Start Somewhere

I don't believe that anything I have written in this book is particularly controversial and I hope that none of it is new. New and clever ways of engaging faith don't appeal to me. However, I have spent enough decades having these conversations to know that pursuing God as Father can make some people uncomfortable.

All of us carry presuppositions, deeply held assumptions that have been formed over time by our families, churches, mentors, traumas, and the culture in which we were raised. Those presuppositions become second nature. They are so familiar to us that we seldom recognize them for what they are: filters through which we listen, process, and accept or reject new information.

Presuppositions serve a valuable purpose. Just imagine the mental energy it would take to process every new piece of information from ground zero, with no conceptual context in which to frame it. How exhausting! Without presuppositions, even the simplest decisions would require enormous expenditures of time and effort. Presuppositions are cognitive shortcuts that make it possible for us to think and act efficiently, but they are not always helpful, because they can also prevent us from truly listening to unfamiliar ideas. And by listening,

I mean REALLY engaging, open to the possibility that an idea that feels threatening to the way we have learned to see the world and understand God might in fact be true.

Our brains are working against us in this, so be nice to yourself. Research has shown that when we are confronted with paradigm-shifting ideas, our brain activity moves from the prefrontal cortex to the amygdala. The prefrontal cortex is that part of our brain that attaches language to our experience, interprets complex concepts, makes decisions, and figures out how best to act in social situations. In other words, it's pretty essential for normal social functioning. The amygdala, on the other hand, is that very instinctual part of our brain that is activated whenever we feel threatened. It sounds an alarm and kicks us into either fighting, running away, or freezing like a deer in the headlights.

Believe it or not, the level of threat our brain feels when our core presuppositions are challenged is the same level it would feel if we were physically attacked. The part of our brain that is responsible for processing information instinctively shuts down when we are under threat, and we go into survival mode. You have seen this every time you've watched a political discussion between two people who passionately hold opposing views. It is obvious to all onlookers, especially those who don't feel their own paradigms threatened, that neither one is actually listening to the other. They are simply viciously defending their core ideas and ideals against the threat posed by the other person's information.

By the way, this is why debating your beliefs is usually a ridiculous idea. Your rhetoric may serve to pump up any other Christians who are within earshot but will rarely help the person you are debating. Faith is a gift. We can't talk people into faith. That's not how faith works. Further, the better your debating skills are, the more threatened the other person will feel and the deeper they will go into that defensive part of their brain, increasing their motivation to fight or run away. If they freeze and stop responding, that doesn't mean you are winning or that they are listening to you. It just means they feel threatened and under attack, and their brain is telling them that if they say nothing and don't move you might go away without causing them harm.

I hope that some of the ideas I'll present in the chapters ahead will prompt you to reexamine your paradigms and presuppositions. That won't be easy, since the prospect of adding to or shifting our beliefs is scary for all of us. So let's begin by acknowledging our attachment to certainty and our natural fear of change. Having done so, let's commit to hanging in there, enduring the discomfort, and trying to stay in that part of our brain that is still listening and engaging.

For the purposes of this book, we can divide ourselves into three basic types of people. Which of these categories best describes you?

The Experienced and Knowledgable Smartass:

I know. I know. I didn't do this group any favors by using the word smartass to describe it. But that was kind of the point. If you are an experienced and learned person, you might have found the term offensive. If you aren't this kind of person, you know others who are, and you smiled knowingly when I used the term. Fear not. I am not without compassion, this is my tribe.

I've grown up in the church. I was steeped in religious education from my earliest experiences through high school, university, and decades in the pulpit. As I understood it, my job as a pastor was to assure people that I had thought through every issue and had found the correct answers. Since I had reached my conclusions, I engaged any new information from a fighting stance. To be completely honest, as I look back I don't even know why I read half the stuff I did. I think that as often as not I just liked winning hypothetical arguments in my mind and growing ever more smug in my certainty.

Experienced and mature friends, I don't want to take a single thing away from your education or your hard-won wisdom. They are gifts. For me, however, the danger came when I no longer needed the Spirit to lead me into truth, because I already had the answers. More than that, I had wrapped up a list of allowable questions. Certain questions were just not okay to engage, and that was sad. Truth is never afraid of honest questions.

If you are a member of this tribe, take a deep breath. There is nothing for you to gain or lose by engaging the simple questions and suggestions in this little book. Your intelligence, your drive to learn, and your years of real-life experience are valuable and beautiful assets, but there is always more to discover. Stay humble, and remember that our Father has given us His Spirit to lead us into all truth.

I'm not asking you to take everything I say at face value. All I'm asking is that you do your best to stay in the conversation. Let's see where this goes.

The Amateur:

Yeah, I picked a name for this tribe that might prick a little. I think it's a little condescending myself. But that is kind of the point. These are the folks who think of themselves as non-professional, amateur Christians. What a lucky group! These were the people Jesus spent a lot of time with and showed so much love for, and this is what I want you to see: the deep truths of the Gospel are for you. According to the gospels, Jesus brought the good news of His Father's kingdom to a peasant culture full of farmers, fishermen, and homemakers more than to the ivory tower theologians in Jerusalem.

I have known too many Christians who feel a constant need to wait for their pastor to explain every subject, and even then are handcuffed by the belief that most of the deep truths of Scripture are beyond them. That is why, if you feel like you fit in this category, I hope that you will not allow me or anyone else to be condescending to you by calling you an amateur. I maintain, by contrast, that any "deep" truth of Scripture that is too complex for the average person in the pew to understand is not the truth of Jesus at all. Such sophisticated and lofty things are sometimes simply human constructs whose primary purpose is to intimidate "the amateurs" into submission by keeping them dazzled and dependent.

Jesus brought the priesthood to all believers. You are not an amateur. You are a priest and an image-bearing child of the Most High. We value those teachers who have been gifted to help lead us in our understanding, but they are not the priests who usher us into the presence of God. Jesus alone does that and His Spirit alone opens our eyes and hearts to truth. Scripture tells us that the natural mind cannot receive Spiritual things, they are Spiritually discerned, and you have God's very Spirit indwelling you my priestly friend.

When it comes to understanding the Gospel, you've got this. You were made for this. My prayer is that I will not err by trying to impress an imaginary jury of religious intellectuals—a jury that would find this book inadequate anyway. Let's just engage in a conversation that is frank, simple, and Gospelicious.

The Skeptic:

If you tend to think that most Christians are a bit nuts, or rather stupid, welcome. You might be a follower of Christ but have been burned by the organized church. I have no idea how you came to pick up this book, but I'm sure it's a great story. It's your story. And right now your story and mine are intersecting. That blows my mind.

You may already be more aware of your presuppositions than others who are reading this book. If so, your skepticism has likely given you permission to engage in "subversive" conversations and challenge accepted beliefs. However, if skepticism has become your primary way of engaging the world, you may be in danger of missing the truth in the same way as the experienced and knowledgeable Christian.

It is possible for skepticism to congeal into a nice jello. Even though the thinking of the skeptic doesn't seem as rigid as that of the Christian whose ideas may be set in dogmatic concrete, at the point they congeal, our so-called "questions" cease to be real questions. They become just another type of dogma in the form of questions. We take on skepticism as an identity rather than a tool in the search for life and truth. So, I invite you to go ahead and read with a shrug. Ask your questions. Field your doubts. Just do your utmost to not become a slave to any of them. I've known far too many skeptics that are miserable in their lives and boring in conversations because they are more dogmatic than some Christians who frustrate me. Some were dear friends and I just wanted them to ask themselves, "How is this working for me?" I personally love your skepticism and hope that you become amazing at using it in a way that is helpful to both you and those people you engage in your life.

Alright. Those are the three basic presupposition groups I'll put forth for your consideration. You may choose to define and join a different group that is more nuanced than the three I listed. If so, fantastic. I only ask that we all take a moment to look inside and try the impossible—to understand the trickiness of our hearts and the degree to which our crazy brain has been fearfully and wonderfully made.

Chapter Three

I See You

Most Christians, regardless of their breed, will come to some agreement on the fact that we are created and redeemed to be in a relationship with our Heavenly Father and one another. Unfortunately, after accepting that fact, many of us move on to other things. The truth of that statement, personal relationship with God, does not penetrate our Christian goals as profoundly as the notion would demand. Paul understood that there was no deeper truth to grasp. He knew that knowing God was the greatest adventure we could embark on.

Near the end of his life, Paul described his most cherished and vital pursuit. In Philippians 3, he wrote that every pursuit in which he had ever engaged and every gain he had ever made was nothing compared to knowing Christ Jesus his Lord. He counted all those things as rubbish. In verse 10 of that chapter, he explained that the righteousness that comes through faith in Christ made it possible for him to know God. He did not claim to have attained perfection but said that he was solely focused on training and striving to know Christ in the power of his resurrection and the fellowship of his sufferings.

Odd isn't it? I'll bet that if we lined up 100 Christians and asked them what their ultimate <u>duty</u> is, few of them would put "knowing God" at the top of the list.

Let's pause to consider the idea of knowing. In our Western world, knowing something usually has academic associations. If I want to know something, I study it. When I can regurgitate the information on a test, I am declared to know it. That kind of "knowing" is not what Paul is talking about in Philippians 3. Paul is not saying, "I have abandoned everything and consider them worthless except for the acquisition of Jesus facts." That's absurd and hardly worth the sentence it took to express, except that what I believe Paul meant in this passage, is not how I naturally tend to approach "knowing" Christ."

Paul is talking about relational knowing. Relational knowing is attached to a person rather than an idea. Studying the Bible and being a brilliant theologian will not automatically cause me to know God. Of course, information is a part of relational knowing (more on that soon), but it is only a part. Paul himself says, in the opening verses of Philippians 3, that he started out by becoming a great Pharisee, a master of religious information, but he draws a distinction between that education and his ultimate pursuit of knowing God. The pure informational part of his journey was a piece of what he counted as rubbish.

In the Hebrew language, the word translated "to know" conveys several different meanings. In Genesis, we read that Adam "knew" Eve and she conceived Cain. Now, if the word "know" simply means connecting mentally, then for me to have a conversation with a woman would be incredibly risky! No, the Hebrew concept of knowing includes intellectual information, intimate interaction, and discovery and perception through experience. That is the kind of knowing that Paul is talking about. He does want to understand God with his mind alone, but he also wants to see Him in creation, feel Him in human relationships, trust Him in the face of life's difficulties, and experience a deep intimate connection with Him in the process. All of that is wrapped up in the power of Jesus' death and resurrection, his participation in that death and resurrection, and sharing in His sufferings. Ironically, when knowing God becomes my chief duty, all other Christian "duties" follow naturally and find a right place that produces freedom and not slavery.

Attaining and retaining knowledge is chasing after the wind if intimacy is not a part of the process. I could seek deeper and deeper knowledge of a wife. I could search out and discover her passions and her pains. I could ask her questions concerning her heart and seek to know every meaningful story from her past. Because I would be in an intimate relationship with her, such a quest for information is not only appropriate, it is beautiful and necessary. The informational knowledge leads to interest, fascination, curiosity, and connection.

Now let's remove the intimacy and leave the pursuit of information. Let's say that I am not married to that woman, there is no intimate personal connection but I seek deeper and deeper knowledge about her. I try to discover her passions and hurts, the stories of her past. I get access to all of her social media pages so I know every move she makes and inspirational memes she shares... you get the picture. The same pursuit of "knowing" is no longer beautiful or appropriate. It is creepy in the extreme. It's called stalking.

Oh, that we would apply what is obvious in life to our relationship with the one we say that we love above all else. In John 17 Jesus says, "This is eternal life, that they know you the only true God, and Jesus Christ whom you have sent."

Jesus does not talk in that passage about eternal life in terms of streets paved with gold, angels, mansions, harps, or choirs. Jesus talks about eternal life in terms of a relationship, in terms of intimate knowledge. Jesus talks about eternal life as something that I can engage in and experience right now. Eternal life does not start when you die, it has already begun. Death is only a transition into a new and wonderful version of your life, but your eternal life journey has already begun.

I do not want to be a creepy Facebook stalker for God. I want to discover what Paul desired so deeply. I want to find that there is nothing sweeter than the love walk with my Daddy. The slow discovery of His heart, His person, and His love for me.

With that, let's talk a little more about knowing God. Our notions about God and His personality are fundamental to our spiritual experience. These ideas shape how we read the Bible and understand it, how we view ourselves, and how we go about our search for Jesus' abundant life. Our ideas about God and His personality are formed over many years by multiple influences, including our family, the church we grew up in (if we went to church), and the culture in which we were raised. They shape our perception of the world, ourselves, and others. More importantly, these foundational ideas can either open or close doors to intimacy with God. In other words, our ideas about God's personality are serious business.

It is common for Christians in all traditions to refer to God as Father, but seldom do we take the time to unpack what that term really means to us personally. For most of us, praying to our "Heavenly Father" or "Father God" is just something that came with the Christian package, a part of the vocabulary. But I have found in my own life and in the lives of those I have served that only by exploring and understanding a clearer view of God as father can we experience the "abundant life" that Jesus promised and find the peace that passes understanding.

The first awkward hurdle we encounter is the challenge of understanding God as a person. When I say person, I don't mean human. I know, it's a word hurdle to get over and you can feel free to pick a better one for yourself, but bear with me. According to scripture, God is not a person with a body. God is Spirit, but He describes himself as an emotional being. In other words, God is not a stoic entity floating somewhere in the ether. This concept is vital for us to grasp. When we ignore His personhood, we reduce God to the purveyor of rules, moral standards, and religious expectations. If God is not a person or an emotional being, then we can make him nothing more than a spreadsheet with fixed formulas, one that automatically connects actions and demands to outcomes without relationship. Doing so is the definition of robbing someone of their personhood.

However, when I remember that God is more than an impersonal force—when I understand that He is an active participant with his creation, complete with a flow of emotions—then I discover a dynamic relationship with God that starts to change my heart. Prayer becomes a conversation, worship becomes intimate, and loving God becomes a reaction to His person rather than a duty. We will discuss some of the dangers of creating God in our own likeness by placing versions of our emotions on Him in a later chapter. But for the moment, let us just agree that God has emotions which He reveals throughout Scripture.

If you are still hung up on God's emotional person, please consider Jesus. Jesus was the fullness of God living a life we can wrap our minds around. No one would accuse Jesus of not being filled with emotions. He wept. He felt lonely. He felt angry. He loved deeply. One of the journeys in this book is to allow God the Father to possess all of the emotions we so easily ascribe to Jesus.

Jesus reaffirmed that the greatest commandment is to love God. You've doubtless heard the phrase "falling in love," and it is an apt description of how love starts. I certainly did not go into relationships "trying" to love. I got to know a person, discovered them, spent time with them, and then love just happened. My heart responded to who they were. We do fall in love, but the maintenance of love requires effort and intention. You fall in love once, but after the fall, you have to climb back into love.

I can never love anyone more than I know them. Knowing someone, a friend or lover is the primary limiting factor in my quest for deeper love. And so it is with God. When I make it my chief practice to seek him, when I make sure to allocate time and effort to that process of discovery, I will inevitably fall in love with Him. How sweet it Is to find that my primary pursuit as a Christian is something as delightful as seeking to discover more about a person who loved me first.

There are metaphors in the Bible and in life that are intended to help us understand our proper relationship with God. For example, God describes his relationship with Israel in marital terms, and in the New Testament, the church is described as Christ's bride. Stay with me here. God created humans and they entered into a familial relationship. He chose that love journey as a way to expose Himself and to help us understand our relationship with Him. God has deliberately chosen marriage as a metaphor to help explain how He acts toward us and feels about us.

So it is with the concept of God as our father. God has allowed all of us to experience being children and has allowed many of us to be parents. Both of those roles help us grasp nuanced and beautiful truths about God. Because I know what the love of a healthy parent looks like, I can understand and believe a piece of God's feelings toward me.

I have had this conversation with thousands of people over the years, and it is not uncommon for someone to tell me that because their own experience with a father or mother was horrible, they will never be able to see God as a loving parent. I have respectfully disagreed. I have found that those who have been wounded the most deeply by parents have a crystal-clear understanding of what a good father or mother should look like, and despite their fear of trusting the journey to know God as father, they have a natural hunger for that deeper relationship with Him. If you are one of those people who have experienced pain in your parental relationships, please know that I empathize with your fear. I understand that there is scar tissue. But take hope. You are in no way handicapped or excluded from this journey. You have everything you need, I promise.

The Zulu tribes of South Africa have the greatest common greeting on the planet. They do not say, "Hello, Gatsha. How are you doing?" They say, "Sawubona, Gatsha," which means, "I see you, Gatsha." Gatsha answers, "Ngikhona, Kagiso," meaning, "I am here, Kagiso."

Within the greeting is the implicit statement of intimacy and knowledge:

"I see you."

"You are an individual."

"I am looking at the heart, the whole you."

If someone greeted me that way and meant it, there would be some degree of vulnerable terror that would rise in me. I, who have been raised in a fairly suppressed emotional culture, might respond by saying, "Well, stop looking!"

Instead, the Zulu responds with:

"I am here."

"I am present for this moment with you."

"I am what you see, no false front or games."

"What you have seen, I am."

This greeting captures the trajectory of our exploration in Soul Architecture. I want to see what God sees and I want to know Him more. I slowly begin to accept that He daily comes to me and smiles. "I see you, Aaron."

When He says the words, my heart leaps within me. I know what He is saying. He sees me, completely, wholly...and holy because of the work of His Son. He does not see me through the lens of the accuser; He sees me through the lens of the cross. "I see you, Aaron."

"Here I am, Daddy," is the return statement, the terrifying confession, the agreement to His terms of my identity.

Here I am. I agree I am complete in Christ. I agree that You see me as Your son without hesitation or reservation. I agree that Jesus' blood has brought me boldly to Your grace even in my dire times of need, sin, shortfalls, and pains, and I am secure. I agree, and I am here.

"Here I am, Daddy."

With bashful reverence, I look up to my Father, knowing that the words I must say can never be entirely true, but He has invited me to say them with what limited knowledge I have. "I see You, Daddy. You are my Father. You are my love and the lover of my soul. This much I see."

Without hesitation, He responds, "Here... I AM."

And that is eternal life.

Chapter Four

Everybody Is a Theologian

Theology is a heady word. It is a word often reserved for pastors and intellectuals. Simply translated it means the "study of God." Practically translated, it is your system of beliefs concerning God's person and thus His behavior in this world and the next. Everyone has a theology. If someone has not studied or been taught to form one, then it will be piecemeal, based on random bits of information that have been gathered throughout their life.

Theology is often discussed and defended in terms of "truthfulness." Too often it is debated as if the purpose of theology is to agree on a perfectly crafted systematic set of ideas, written down and dispatched to the masses. However, theology for theology's sake is simply an arrogant hobby. As we discussed, the pursuit of understanding or "knowing" the person of God is far more personal than that.

When used well, good theology is like a balloon being filled with air. The bigger my view of God, the more pieces of truth that fall into place, the bigger the balloon gets. The space within can create space to move and to live the abundant life. If I know little of God through the light of His Word and His creation, the space in which I can move and live is limited. The voice of God's character and His heart for my life will be anemic and small. However, as my understanding increases, my potential for applying His love and feelings in my life also increases.

I say "potential" for living because in my practical life, what I say I believe does not matter if I still act and react based on false stories in my head about my identity and the world I live in. Such false stories create warped versions of the theology I have come to believe. I can read all of the Augustine, Aquinas, Berkhof, Grudem, or Hodge that I want. I can agree to all of the information held within their covers. But when the rubber meets the road, I will live out what I genuinely believe. I will FEEL what I believe.

There is one more piece to this balloon analogy, and it is an important one. The systematizing of theology has been both a blessing and a curse over the last 2,000 years. It is indeed a blessing because it organizes majestic thoughts and themes into digestible pieces, and since our beliefs about God is so important in shaping our lives, we say thank you.

Many people, however, have tied the knot on their "balloon." When they find a system of theological thoughts that they feel comfortable and confident in, they close the cover and accept that the balloon is properly inflated. There is no more access for the Spirit's breath or surprise, to push the boundaries out, and anything that asks that person to allow for more filling is held in suspicion. But oh how Jesus loved to push the boundaries out. He kept "blowing air" into His disciples until they were sure the whole thing would pop - but it never did.

Some folks might feel concerned with that idea. They might feel that leaving my balloon unknotted will allow for bad theology to enter my mind and heart. Yup. Totally true. But consider these two things. First, if I listen to that fear and tie my balloon off, I am practically stating that I believe that everything I have come to believe IS true, and all the truth that is out there to know. That what I have read in books written by people and sermons preached by humans has all led to right conclusions. There is nothing left to be fixed or nuances to be added.

I don't believe that. Heck, I can guarantee you that not all of what I have written in this book is perfectly accurate. To claim that would be insane. So leaving my balloon open gives me the opportunity to remove wrong thinking as much as it allows space for the Holy Spirit to fill me with something new.

Second, if anyone has that fear, know that you are not alone. People in Jesus' day had the same fear - ABOUT JESUS. You probably remember Jesus saying, "You have heard it said...but I say," six times in the sermon on the mount alone. He said it as an unknotting of balloons when He taught. "You have heard it said." This is the old way of seeing this. "But I say..." I'm about to take what you thought you understood and blow your mind. There is more. Wait for it. Ready? Jesus' unknotting of theological balloons is like that moment before stepping off a high diving board for the first time, or the feeling of a jet accelerating as it begins to thrust you into flight. It is thrilling.

Jesus gets to do that. He's Jesus. But even when Jesus did it, His words to us get filtered through the minds, hearts, and interpretations of those people teaching on Jesus' teaching. I highly recommend that you don't let any human system of theology rob you of the ongoing journey of discovery in your relationship with God. I wish we had one of those black lights they use in crime scenes or some fingerprint dusting kit when we listen to any teaching. Something that could show us exactly how many human fingerprints are plastered across everything divine. Mind you, those finger prints do not make a teaching wrong, just that we are never consuming the pure thing.

We must pause to confess that this is a very hard truth. I know many "learned" women and men who will not even entertain this conversation because they have not experienced practical "transformation" in their lives, even though they believe their theology is in order. There is an underlying fear that the truths they believe may not be enough. The unspoken fear is that either they failed or God has failed. In either case, most of us would rather go on *talking* about the "truth" and theology that we are supposed to believe than addressing the fear that those truths have fallen short in our actual experience.

Let me make something very clear. I do not believe that such a person is lying, or that they do not deeply believe in what they have come to know as truth. I do not believe there is a person on earth who is living out all that they say they believe, not in total harmony with the eternal facts of the immutable God. I know I certainly fall short of that. Apart from Jesus, the integration of our beliefs into experience is impossible.

However, I believe that when we are not seeing our lives, behaviors, and feelings transformed by the truths we believe, our beliefs and theology get cheapened to an all-important status. Life has been left behind and replaced with a desk and chair in an ivory tower. We believe it and become satisfied with that fact alone. I'm not OK with that. If the truths I believe are not making any practical difference in my life and relationships then I want to go back to the drawing board and see what I must be missing.

If you have found that you talk a good game in your small group but can't stop grieving your actual experience when you try to sleep at night, take hope. Don't be afraid to face the areas of your life that seem to remain stuck in a rut even though you know the verses that should have winched you out of those holes years ago. Face them with courage because your theology profoundly matters. The truth that the Holy Spirit leads us into does transform.

As you form a clearer view of God's character and His Gospel, and you begin to apply it practically to the lies that run rampant in your mind, you will see change. Your theology will become real and active. First comes understanding, then true belief enlivened by the Spirit. Then those truths that have been laid as a foundation in your soul will become your bulwark against the crashing tide of false and accusing stories in your life because God's truth will be more powerful than the accuser's lies.

Such a journey cannot be taken in a class or from reading a book. It can start there, but it cannot be completed. That is the lie of the Western educational mindset that we talked about earlier. Learning the information is only the first step.

Do you believe that God is Sovereign, in control? Then how does that truth shape today's fear regarding bills that are coming up? Do you believe that God is your Abba and His love endures forever? Then how does that truth change the pain of betrayal or abuse that plagues your heart? Do you believe in the substitutionary atonement of the Christ on Calvary's cross? Then how does that eternal fact affect your shame today when you slip into familiar sin and see a Holy God seated upon mercy's throne?

Oh, how your theology, how you see God, matters! The larger your view of God, the higher your quotient for freedom and abundant life. Let no man speak of bland platitudes while his life languishes in the shadow of his flesh. Theology was meant to be lived, and we seek to live it.

Above all remember this: In John 14, Jesus said, "I am the truth." All truth will end in a face-to-face encounter. A truth divorced from the person of Jesus is either incomplete or wrong. Like Paul, we seek to know Christ in the power of His resurrection and the fellowship of His sufferings. As we find Him, we discover that Jesus is not just the truth, but He is the way, and the life as well.

Chapter Five

It's Far Worse Than We Thought

In the physical world, one's understanding of sickness directly affects the kind of treatment they seek. If we believe a pain is simply a headache, we go to the medicine cabinet and take a Tylenol. However, if we discover the same pain is a tumor, we take a different approach. Genius, I know.

The nature of our fallenness, the sin we live in, is very much like that. For the most part, Christians have attached the idea of symptoms to the problem of sinfulness: "I struggle with lust," "She is a gossip," or "That guy committed adultery." We look at the outward expression of fallenness and then write a prescription. This is called "sin management." If we manage the sin, we will then be all right. Unfortunately, sin management and transformation are not the same things.

The real problem is far worse than we see on the surface. The sins we are drawn toward or indulge in are only the external symptoms of a much deeper problem. We have been saturated in fallenness, surrounded by it. Thus the best we can do is pick out the peaks of the icebergs, as their cold heads peer at us through the surface of our lives. But beneath the surface, the real monster sits in silent darkness.

In Eden, God tells us of a tree and the first fall into sin. In that story, in that fruit, we find the seeds of every fallen fruit we have been tempted to taste. This is our broken heritage:

"And out of the ground the LORD God made to spring up every tree that is pleasant to the sight and good for food. The tree of life was in the midst of the garden, and the tree of the knowledge of good and evil. The LORD God took the man and put him in the Garden of Eden to work it and keep it. And the LORD God commanded the man, saying, 'You may surely eat of every tree of the garden, but of the tree of the knowledge of good and evil you shall not eat, for in the day that you eat of it you shall surely die.' Now the serpent was more crafty than any other beast of the field that the LORD God had made. He said to the woman, "Did God actually say, 'You shall not eat of any tree in the garden'?" And the woman said to the serpent, "We may eat of the fruit of the trees in the garden, but God said, 'You shall not eat of the fruit of the tree that is in the midst of the garden, neither shall you touch it, lest you die.'"

"But the serpent said to the woman, 'You will not surely die. For God knows that when you eat of it your eyes will be opened, and you will be like God, knowing good and evil.' So when the woman saw that the tree was good for food, and that it was a delight to the eyes, and that the tree was to be desired to make one wise, she took of its fruit and ate, and she also gave some to her husband who was with her, and he ate. Then the eyes of both were opened, and they knew that they were naked. And they sewed fig leaves together and made themselves loincloths. " (Gen. 2:9, 15-17, 3:1-7)

Was it a magical fruit that changed the spiritual property of man? What actually happened that day? No one can say for certain. One shift is sure, however. God is painting a picture and giving us a glimpse into mankind beginning to make their own judgments apart from God.

I was taught as a kid that the root of all sin is pride. That may be so, but it comes in the form of judgment, to make a choice, or to appraise something apart from God's valuation. God's clear statement concerning the significance of the tree was that it was harmful, it was bad for them. He told them the day they ate it, they would die. He did not say that He would kill them, just that, "they would surely die." If they lived within the harmony of a world built on His judgment, they would have lived in peace, without shame, with nothing to hide.

In Chapter Three of Genesis, a shift occurred. Adam and Eve made a choice, an evaluation, a judgment for themselves. Eve saw that it looked good, seemed tasty, and wanted the knowledge that she believed she would gain from it. Adam saw that she was eating it and decided that he couldn't live without her and he ate it. Choices. Their own choices.

Independence came to man, oh celebrated freedom. The serpent's temptation to Eve implied that God was not good, that He was withholding something. He said the tree would make them wise, not kill them. Thus, they judged that God's warning was not valid, or at least not as weighty as He was making it out to be, and they ate, and everything changed.

I don't know if it was a magical fruit. I don't think it had to be. I think it could have been a rock or a stick on the ground that God said, "Don't pick it up or you will die." Of course, that would have wrecked the symmetry of the two special trees in the garden, but you get the point. The desperate shift in humanity, the fallenness, the pride, is that mankind now struggles to trust God's goodness and judgments in everything. We pit our evaluations about what is better for ourselves against walking in simple Edenic faith where God's valuation ruled.

Isn't it interesting that after they ate the fruit, Scripture tells us that their eyes were opened? They saw they were naked. They covered themselves because they were ashamed, and then they hid from God. What a list of consequences!

Their eyes were opened. Don't miss the weirdness of that statement, it's easy to gloss over. Even our judgment of the statement, "open eyes" proves that we judge backward now. Going into something with our "eyes open," means we have investigated, we have discerned, we approach a thing with wisdom. It's a good thing. On the flip side, to do a thing "blindly," means we haven't thought it through. The consequences are easy for everyone else to see but we are going to do it anyways. So in our cultural estimation, open eyes are good, and closed eyes are bad. Yet here in the garden, the first consequence of eating the fruit was to have their eyes opened. They saw for themselves. They had their own knowledge of good and evil. The promise of the fruit proved true.

The following verses tell us what that meant. Their eyes were opened and they made their first solo judgment post-fruit salad. They were ashamed of being naked. They decided that it was a shameful thing. God had not deemed it bad or shameful. God had made it so and it was good. What He created as good, they now judged as bad. They took that judgment and moved to action based on it. They covered themselves. They disordered God's order. He made them naked and they physically altered his garden ways.

Because of all of that, they hid from God. Our judgments apart from God's values lead to our emotional isolation in shame, to physical acts of doing things our own way, and then to a relational feeling of separation from God. Take careful note that in that moment in the garden it was not God withdrawing from man because of their sin, it was man who withdrew from God. Immediately after this episode, we

find God moving toward them, inviting them to relational reconciliation through confession. More on that later, but for now, see how
it all started with making judgments for ourselves and the inevitable
consequences to our hearts and lives.

Consider how many judgments we make every day. That outfit is
ugly...That car is amazing...The perfect life would be to have a husband
who will take care of me, and have three kids and a house that we
own...Those people are sick...Those people are stupid...I need a better
job...I am ugly or unattractive. Evaluations and judgments, all day,
every day. We think most of them are benign. They are not. They
might not be immoral, but they are not benign. How many of our
thoughts come from our intimate walk with my Lord? Who taught
us those things that we automatically believe without a conscious
process? Often, no one told me - I just learned them through experiences and my judgments of those experiences. They flow from Adam's
blood that courses through my veins.

Don't misunderstand. I'm not judging your preferences. There is
no moral problem with liking one color more than another. But we
must separate out the idea of my judgments and my preferences. I
desperately want us to feel the weight of our complete saturation in
self-judgment (judging for ourselves, not judging ourselves). We bathe
in it daily. It soaks us to our core.

That is not the world we once occupied with our Creator. He once
told us what was amazing and desirable. We took our cues from His
heart and His mind. Now, even that which is trivial represents my
plucking from the tree, valuations I choose for myself. My day is filled
with the proof of my own rebellion. My brokenness is far deeper than
the manifestations of sin that crawl up to the surface of my life. Sin
is not just looking at pornography, yelling at the kids, or speaking

inappropriately about someone when they are not around. It is the very state I am in as a child of the first Adam.

Let me give you an innocuous example of how this works practically. I was on a drive with someone heading north from Santa Barbara and we were talking about these thoughts on judging for ourselves. We were stuck in traffic and there was a white panel van next to us. It was a work van, there might have been ladders on top. I asked, "What do you think of that van?" Without hesitations, she said something like, "I don't know, it's fine I guess. I wouldn't want it. It's ugly."

OK. All right. That's fair. It wasn't a fancy vehicle. It was a utilitarian item, not a luxury or sports vehicle meant to turn heads.

I then asked, "What do you think God thinks about it?"

"God?"

"Sure, why not? Does God not get to have opinions about panel vans?

We then spent the next hour-and-a-half talking about possible answers to that question based on what we knew about God throughout the Bible. Here are a few scenarios I can remember.

"Maybe he would think about the first person to take the automobile and create something that could be useful in a different way. I don't know their name, but God would. Maybe he would remember when the thought came to their mind and how they worked that thought until he or she brought something into the world that would be used for generations after they were gone. God must have enjoyed watching His precious kid being creative and practical, using the gifts that had been placed in their mind and hands. Maybe when he looks at that van He smiles and thinks of that person. He must love vans."

We ended up being alongside that van for quite a while and we saw that the driver was Hispanic. I remembered friends from a restaurant I worked at in Los Angeles when I was younger. There were a number of men who worked in the back who would hang out and play softball with me from time to time. Every one of them worked at least two jobs and sent half of their money back home to their families in Mexico. Now, obviously, I had a small test group on this and I don't assume their story is everyone's story, but the driver of that van made me think of them.

"I wonder who that guy is. God knows. He knows if this is his van for a business he owns and how proud and excited he must have felt when he purchased it. How his heart must have swelled because of what he was about to get to do with it. He also knows if he is just working for someone else, working hard but still having to work other jobs because he wants to help his family far away. Man God must love that guy."

I remember tearing up so many times talking about that van and what God might say if I was able to ask him what his judgment on it was. What is it that he valued about it? When I think of worship, that is one of the first examples that comes to mind. A conversation about a white panel van on the 101 freeway.

Notice a couple of things. First, we were making everything up about the van and the guy. We had no real information about those things. We did, however, have a lot of information about the heart of God. Jesus gave it to us throughout his life. Letting God have a voice in the conversation did not give us divine information about a thing, it simply turned our eyes to Him. And if you noticed from those two examples, we could not conjure any hypothesis about how God felt about the van itself, it always came back to how much He loves His kids.

The result of that conversation? We fell in love with God just a little bit more. Oh, and she decided she liked that white panel van.

I hope that helped to clarify that we make snap judgments all the time that aren't morally wrong, they just exclude any notion that God might have an opinion that would change the entire conversation. We will talk more about the practicals of that in the last chapter of this book. Let's get back to how making our judgments on our own affects us.

Every manifestation of sin represents something I have judged as lacking in my life and my attempt to self-soothe or fill that perceived void.

Does that make sense? My favorite sins are always connected to something that I don't trust God's judgment on. People who use substances don't do it just because it is fun and often continue to do it long after it makes them miserable. Why? The stories behind the "why" will vary but they will all come down to a central point where that person felt that something hurt too much, something was unmanageable, emotions were too strong. Even a story that might include a path of drug use that started with something as simple as peer pressure in High School has that same core power thrumming beneath the surface. What is peer pressure? It is a sense of not being enough or a fear of being rejected or ridiculed if one does not go with the crowd. Why am I not enough? Why am I in danger of ridicule? Whatever my answer is at that moment is a judgment upon my identity that is light years away from God's evaluation. But in believing my judgment I take a step into the manifestation of that judgment which is a behavior. That behavior becomes a habit and ultimately reinforces the judgment. And the wheel begins to spin.

I have been with Christians who believe they take sin very seriously. What that has always meant is that they have a clear list of behaviors that they will call people out on. I personally think that is a very shallow view of sin that will not lead to heart transformation. I want to understand the depth of my disconnection with God so that I can understand the depth of my salvation... so that I can reconnect with God... so that I don't simply have to power through sin management. I want my behavior to improve because my judgments and behaviors have lost their flavor and living in God's love through the person and work of Christ is increasingly sweet.

Fear not, dear reader, for this is not the end; it is only the beginning. Remember, if your headache is more than a headache, you want to know about it so that you can get the proper care. Until we understand that our lives are absolutely unmanageable and that our self-judgment is running completely unacknowledged, we will continue to attempt to manage the symptoms, rather than treat the cause.

Our hope, our only hope, is more than sin management. The hope of the Gospel is rebirth, a return to hearing the Spirit's voice in the garden. Experiencing re-creation.

Chapter Six

Those Crazy Christians

Have you ever wondered how in the world some people think the way they do? I used to amuse myself during my 30-minute drive to work in the mornings by flipping between the super liberal AM radio station and the super conservative AM radio station. They would be reporting the exact same news stories every day, but their coverage could not have been more different in conclusions or perspectives.

Most of us have listened to someone passionately defend how they see the world and we think, "They can't possibly believe what they are saying." But I believe that they do. I believe that people have insanely different ways of seeing things and that opposing views can be seen with equal conviction.

God has created our minds in a spectacularly exciting way. We are not like other animals, whose reality is based on basic instincts and raw data. They seek food, water, protection, and a mate to survive and continue their species. It's simple for them. Not necessarily easy, but simple. Reality for us is not based on facts and data alone but rather the perceptions of facts. Let me illustrate.

FOX aired a sitcom some years back called, "Malcolm in the Middle." Malcolm was a genius kid growing up in a dysfunctional family. At the beginning of one episode, he was sitting watching television with two of his brothers and his older brother commented on the program's statement concerning the speed of shuttles in outer space. He thinks the show must be wrong because if you went that fast you wouldn't float around like he's seen, you'd be pinned to your seat.

Malcolm responds. "You're confusing acceleration with velocity. ...once you're up to speed, you don't even notice. I mean, right now, we're on a planet that's spinning one thousand miles per hour, and that's just rotational velocity. We're also traveling around the sun at almost 67,000 miles per hour. And then, the whole solar system is hurtling around the galaxy which is hurtling away from all of the other galaxies because the universe is expanding."

Two interesting things happen at that point. First, Malcolm's brothers' perspectives change. They thought they were sitting still, sitting on a couch in their living room. The introduction of new data disrupted their paradigm or the way they saw the world. What happened after that, however, is far more important.

Upon receiving this new information, Malcolm's older brother begins to look uncomfortable. Slowly he reaches up to the arm of the sofa and grips it for some stability. Malcolm's little brother ponders the same information and says, "Whee!"

Same data, two different ways to perceive the information. One brought terror; the other brought a new thrill and joy to life. This is the gift of the "transformation of the mind." It is not just the data, but how we perceive that data, that determines the "reality" that we practically experience.

Take five children, in five different homes, each suffering the same trauma at the same age. Let's say they experience sexual abuse at age eight. That is the fact, the data. That is what happened to them, full stop. If their reality was based solely on the fact of that experience, then one would expect all five children to end up in the same place as adults. We could chart and predict their trajectory, but it is not so.

Child one might become incredibly protective of children because of what happened to him and child two an abuser himself. The story child three could hear and believe in his mind might be one of worthlessness, that he is forever broken. Child four might have a righteous anger against such crimes. He becomes aware of those who lure children as he was preyed upon as a child. He becomes active in his community and his family to make sure that what happened to him will never happen to another child who lives within his protective gaze. Child five might struggle with his sexual identity and experience confusion about whether the abuse was his fault or if he enjoyed it. We could go on and on listing hypothetical places that those five children landed as adults and we could see how each of them could experience a combination of many of those stories.

Those thoughts, or narratives, were also shaped by whether the children kept it a secret or the reactions of those they may have told. All of those thoughts, all of the stories move that child into a "reality." The story after the data creates a filter through which the data is strained, what comes out of the other side becomes their perspective, and that perspective informs action throughout their lives. That is what I mean by reality. We all experience it. We all have filters that have been formed by our experiences and our past. What comes out on the other side of those filters is how we see the world and those "life goggles" we look through justify or motivate our behaviors.

We have all known people who have walked through sickness. Some do it with grace and courage, while some do not. We know people who have suffered loss; some have lost their faith, while others have grown in their faith. What is the difference? Those people have had the same basic experiences, but they have come to very different conclusions.

If this is still feeling wishy-washy to you, consider this. The Harvard Gazette posted an article in which participants were shocked by another participant under intentional and unintentional conditions.[1] This was the second such experiment I had heard of and they both resulted in the same conclusion. When participants believed that pain was intentional they rated the pain as being significantly worse than those who experienced what they thought was accidental pain.

The raw data was the same for all participants but the experience was not. The shocks were the same. But even pain runs through our filters and as anyone who has been betrayed can tell you, there is a difference in how pain feels when we believe we were hurt intentionally. However, what if you believed you were betrayed and it turned out to be a misunderstanding? Our perception changes the reality we experience and sometimes that reality gets slippery and murky.

At the core, there is the same underlying question the serpent brought to bear in the garden when he tempted Eve to eat the fruit. "Is God really good, or is He withholding goodness from you?" How we answer that question, and what we believe in our darkest times of fear and suffering most often dictates the "realities" we live in.

We like to believe that it is not so. It's easier to believe that what we experience is simply about the "things" that happened. It's safer to believe we are victims of circumstance, that we have a right to all of our emotional outbursts and self-absorption when we find ourselves in crisis, and I am not going to argue that point. I am, however, saying that God has created a world in which we participate in the creation process through the perception of those experiences that we have had. I have come to believe that there is a vital Gospel reason that God has made us that way.

---

1. https://news.harvard.edu/gazette/story/2008/12/pain-is-more-intense-when-inflicted-on-purpose/

In Romans 12:2, Paul writes, "Do not be conformed to the world (or take it as your mold), but be transformed by the renewing of your mind." Those words come on the heels of him calling us to live in light of God's mercy, His sacrifice, His drawing us toward Him through the sacrifice of His Son, and then us laying down our lives on His altar as our act of worship. As we live in that way, always in light of His Gospel story, we begin to see a transformation. We experience a transformation of our minds and as a result, a transformation of our realities.

That transformation causes us to interpret the data of our lives differently. Suffering begins to look different than it did when we were not living in view of His love and grace. Paul's perspective on his suffering is insane to most people when we read his words without giving them a Sunday School gloss. He was living in a Gospel reality. The world he occupied was not the same world that most others trod. He walked in the Kingdom.

The word for transformation used in Romans 12 is the same word used when Jesus was transformed before Peter, James, and John in Matthew 17:2. "And he was transfigured before them, and his face shone like the sun, and his clothes became white as light."

That transformation happens in us as we draw closer to the presence of God, like Moses on the mountain receiving the law. "And we all, with unveiled face, beholding the glory of the Lord, are being transformed into the same image from one degree of glory to another. For this comes from the Lord who is the Spirit." (2 Corinthians 3:18)

Transformation is the working out of the Gospel in our lives. The word "Gospel" is most often used in the context of a salvation message. I believe that the Gospel is the hope of sanctification as much as it is the power of God for salvation. In other words, if I throw out my need for the Gospel after salvation, then I am as foolish as the Galatian church, who began by the power of the Spirit but then thought they could live out their faith by their own effort (Gal. 3:3).

When the Gospel work begins to take root, the transformation of my mind is vital. It is a radical thing that takes all of my present situations and relationships, all of my struggles and passions, and redeems them through the lens of the cross and the love and mercy of Christ. Where I walked with bitterness and frustration, I now begin to experience faith, hope, and love. The eternal gold of the Kingdom begins to shine in my actual experiences.

Even more miraculous, the transformation is retroactive. It is not only effective to change the data of today and hope for tomorrow, but the data and stories of the past change as well. What is my past? A combination of curated memories that I have attached significance or stories to. The past is all in my mind, it's not still happening. What does the Gospel claim to have the power to do? Transform my mind. The stories of my past are still subject to running through the same filters that the data from my present go through. If they are shame filters, I will continue to feel shame every time I run those thoughts through my mind. But oh when those memories find a new filter in Christ!

Those pieces of my life that caused me deep shame, I now find a new story that accepts my Daddy's forgiveness and acceptance. The hurts and villainous pains that others had inflicted upon me begin to morph into glorious and inexplicable vistas of grace and forgiveness. The facts of my past don't change but how I perceive them start to look and feel incredibly different.

Every Christian has heard sermons on forgiveness and laying down bitterness. We have heard how dangerous it is to carry those burdens through life. I would contend that there is no real forgiveness you or I can offer apart from a Gospel-transformed mind that is miraculously changing the shape of the story through the lens of the cross. When that kind of forgiveness happens, despite me, it occurs wholly because of Christ.

The Gospel is the lens through which we have been offered to perceive the world. We can't fake that. That is the working out of our salvation. But when that lens is in place, we see today differently, our hope for the future looks different, and when we look back over the landscape of our past, the Gospel changes how I see my failures and the hurts that others have caused me. We were uniquely created for the Gospel to change reality without necessitating the data to change at all.

This is what a Gospel-centered Christian looks like walking in a fallen world. In one word, they look crazy. A reasonable person who does not subscribe to biblical thinking could classify what I just wrote as a kind of dissociative disorder. They might explain it away as a mental tool in which a sick person disconnects from their pain, trauma, or shame and leaps into a different identity or reality so that they can deal or cope with life. Yup. I can't argue with someone who feels that way. I get it.

So, is the Gospel an excuse for some kind of dissociative disorder? Is it all just spiritual bypass? Listen, friend, everyone lives in a reality based on the perception and judgment of the facts of their lives. The atheist does it, the agnostic does it, the Muslim does it, and the Buddhist does it. Everyone has a paradigm that they believe, through which they interpret the facts of their lives. As they interpret their lives through their filters, it shapes how they emotionally and mentally experience the data of their physical experience.

The real question is, what do you believe? Most Christians have verbally confessed to the tenets of the Christian faith, but have we lived what Romans 12:1-2 would call a life-and-mind transformative experience? If someone wants to call a Christian who lives and loves in light of the Gospel unrealistic because they see life in such an otherworldly way, then I say let them. Isn't that what people are supposed to see in Christians everywhere? That they just don't see the world in the same way as the rest of the people around them?

The way you perceive life is the reality you will live. Period. And it's God's fault. And it's wonderfully hopeful.

Chapter Seven

I Reckon, I Oughta

Throughout this book, we will be using the word "reckon" to define a state of Gospel living that transcends simple Christian club membership or mental agreement to the tenets of the Christian dogmas and doctrines. In Romans 6, Paul says, "The death He (Jesus) died he died to sin, once for all, but the life he lives he lives to God. So you also must consider yourselves dead to sin and alive to God." (v. 10-11)

The word he uses in verse 11 for "consider," is sometimes translated as "count," or "reckon." It is the Greek word, logízomai. It is the root of our English word, logic or logical. To "reckon" something is to come to a logical conclusion, an absolute bottom line. The phrase, "bottom line" is an accounting term, referring to the bottom of the ledger. Calculations are made, added, and subtracted, and those totals equal a final statement of truth. That is the definition of the word "reckon."

All of that sounds technical and can feel heady and even convoluted in its practical outworking, but it is not. The process of reckoning happens naturally and intuitively in many areas of our lives all of the time. It is the process by which something goes from being "true" to being "real." Examples of this phenomenon abound.

I cherish the memories of my children's grand entrances into our family. My first came by way of an unexpected pregnancy. I recall the doctor telling me that my wife's blood test proved a fact that I could not see. She was pregnant. At that moment, I believed the truth of her condition, but I had no idea how shallow the reality of it was to me. As I write this very paragraph, I am sitting with that same son at a coffee shop while he works on his schoolwork, and I can say that my reality has increased significantly since that day. As her belly grew, reality grew. I heard the "whush, whush, whush," of the heartbeat, and reality increased. I saw an ultrasound, a picture of the actual child, and I believed with a different kind of certitude. Then came a day when I touched and smelled and kissed him for myself, and on that day, I reckoned the truth that I had always believed. It became real.

There was never a time that I did not "believe" the truth. My belief was just small, and though I thought it changed my life, little had actually changed. It was a beautiful beginning, but there was far more to come.

As I move into the Gospel becoming reckoned in my life, I come to actively believe what is written at the "bottom line" in the ledger of my story. I draw from that account because I do not believe that the books were cooked. I don't believe that my faith is simply a crutch or a nice idea, I don't believe it represents truth, it is simply real.

Some may worry about this additional complexity of "reckoning" in their spiritual life. It may cause them to wonder, "Have I reckoned the Gospel? Am I saved if I haven't yet?" Friend, relax. God tells us to "Believe on the Lord Jesus Christ and you will be saved." For, "he who has the Son has life." Do not burden yourself on the journey to engage your great hope but rather prepare yourself for the joy of more to come. As the Gospel is reckoned more deeply, such doubts will inevitably go away.

The next few chapters will lay out what I believe to be God's ledger of hope and redemption concerning our identities in Christ, but those are only words. "Reckoning" will require something more.

I was speaking with a young friend of mine many years ago, and he was expressing frustration with a theology class he was taking. It was a class full of "right" answers, but he looked around at the lives of the people in his class and knew that the right answers were not affecting many of them practically. So what was the point? A reasonable and profound question that we have touched on in earlier chapters.

That same week I had been reading "Frankenstein," and at that moment with my young friend, a thought occurred to me: our didactic, information-oriented church teaching is not so different from the work of Victor Frankenstein. He laid out the "raw materials" just as we do. The answers we have received have all of the components for a Gospelicious life. They are indeed powerful, but we cannot animate them. Just as Victor needed a power outside of himself to bring life to the raw materials. He used electricity. We wait on and pray for the Holy Spirit to do what only the Spirit can.

"The person without the Spirit does not accept the things that come from the Spirit of God but considers them foolishness, and cannot understand them because they are discerned only through the Spirit." (1 Corinthians 2:14)

The work of the Holy Spirit does not end with conversion. He continues to teach and apply God's words to our hearts. He "quickens" us, or brings life to us. Arthur Pink put it like this in his book on the Holy Spirit. "In His work of illumination, conviction, conversion, and sanctification, the Spirit uses the Word as the means thereto, but in His initial work of 'quickening' He employs no means, operating immediately or directly upon the soul. First there is a "new creation"

(2 Cor. 5:17; Eph. 2:10), and then the "new creature" is stirred into exercise."[1]

We don't know when and how the Spirit will do what the Spirit will do in our hearts. The first time I acted like a reckoned son of God was decades after I had come to Christ. I finally realized that I had significantly limited the Gospel, relegating it to only a position of salvific power. Thus, the Gospel held nothing for me but a sweet memory of conversion. The rest was up to me. I called that discipline and discipleship. That's how I understood Christian maturity, but I discovered I was not reading the Bible very well.

I began to study and pray and meditate on the true Gospel, the Gospel for living, for sanctification, not only salvation. Then one day, I sinned. My usual response to sin would have been shame, perhaps anger with a side order of self-pity. But not that day, for the Spirit had other plans. Immediately I cried out to God. Literally cried out. These were my words, "God, deal with this crap. I am so sick of this nonsense."

I closed my mouth, startled by my outburst, and then it struck me. My emotion, my heart, had connected my sin to something other than...me. I sided with my Abba and cried out for His hand of strength against my flesh that was, at that very moment, seeking to undo me. I believed in my identity in Christ more than my identity in the flesh. I pulled the car over on the side of the freeway. I was crying too hard to drive. I wouldn't have known it the day before, but I knew at that moment it was the first time I had ever <u>felt</u> saved.

---

1. Pink, Arthur W.. The Holy Spirit (Arthur Pink Collection Book 34) . Prisbrary Publishing. Kindle Edition.

I wish that we could control how and when we reckon the Gospel, but we cannot. Just as the first believers were sent to wait and pray, so we wait and pray. We fix our eyes on Christ; we dwell on the truth of the Gospel that brings us a new identity, and then we let the Spirit do what the Spirit does.

As you read on, when you see the word "reckoned," do not take it lightly. It is not a small word. It is a piece of our glorious hope for practical Kingdom living in this fallen world. Because of Jesus' work, we get to reckon the heart freedom, and shame-crushing truth, I am dead to sin and alive in Christ.

Chapter Eight

Learning My Name

"And God said, 'let there be...'" God spoke and His words created worlds. Did you know that you have been endowed with that power? Your words create worlds.

That sounds a bit over the top, but it's really not. We already talked about how our perceptions end up being the reality we embody as we move through our day. What shapes our perceptions? A few things, but few of them are as powerful as words. Even the data/experiences of my day can be shaped by words.

For example, say that I worked all weekend on a project for work, but when I present it at the office on Monday it gets shot down. That's the data. That is simply what happened. Now consider that my manager comes up and tells me, "Man, I'm so sorry that didn't work out. I know you worked really hard on it last weekend and I'm so disappointed they decided to go a different way with it. It was really great." Would that change how I felt and experienced the data? Now consider that my manager comes up to me and says, "Geez man, what were you thinking? That was the dumbest idea I've ever heard. I'm so sick of dealing with you." You get the picture. Words create worlds.

I had a dear friend who, in his 50s was still struggling because of brutal verbal bullying he experienced in elementary school. It blew my mind. But then I considered how many memories still remain vivid in my mind from times when I was teased or torn down as a child. Those examples I gave are of how our words to each other create worlds that can carry impacts for better or worse for decades. As a side note, this is why I hate sarcastic humor in friend groups that pick on individuals. Often the perpetrators of such humor will say something like, "Aw, that's just how we act with each other. They know it's just a joke." Nope, that's not how it works. Words create worlds.

If words to one another can have such weighty impacts, consider how many words you use about yourself. They might be words you think or the way you tell stories about yourself to other people. You might employ self-deprecating humor or feel you are being "really honest" by making sure to point out your faults, but what do those words actually do to your soul?

Can you think of any not-so-nice phrases that you have told yourself or others that start with "I'm?" For example, "I'm fat." "I'm stupid." "I'm not good at anything." "I'm unlovable." "I'm ugly." "I'm an alcoholic." "I'm a horrible parent." "I'm broken."

I want you to take a moment and list some of the most pervasive "I'm" statements that have been at the back or front of your mind throughout your life. Write them down before you move on. Take a few breaths and run your mind and heart back to find some of those phrases.

Hang with me on this rabbit trail dear friends, I promise that my purpose will become clear. John Walton has written some interesting books about functional vs. material ontology. Ontology is the study of existence. What is the nature of being? He explores the mindset of the ancient biblical world concerning what makes something real. I recommend you look him up if you want a far more complete version of what I will present in the next few paragraphs.

To us, and the way we have been taught to think in our material ontology, a thing is real because it is physical, I can touch it, I see it. It can also be real because I hear it. I engage a thing with one of my senses and thus I know it is real. Because I naturally think that way, it is hard for me to take seriously the idea that my words create worlds. Words are just words.

Ancient Near Eastern cultures had a different mindset. A thing could be a thing, but it was not yet "real" until it was separated out, named, and given a function or a purpose. A thing is more than a sum of its parts. That does not mean Jews didn't understand physicality, or that if they saw and touched something that hadn't been ordered and made functional and named they were just in confusion. "I see it there but I'm just not sure, maybe it's not there, I just can't know, hurry, someone order it and name it, I'm going out of my mind." It is simply a very different filter that they had. When I understand that, it makes certain things clearer in the Old Testament. But I must stop reading Scripture as if those writers three and four thousand years ago think through the same filters I do.

Take the table in my dining room. Sure, it's wood, has a top, has legs, but it's more than a wood top and leggy thing. It serves as a gathering space for loved ones, a game space to play cards with the kids, and a temporary depository for mail to get dumped on. A material understanding focuses on the thing itself, but the functional understanding takes into consideration far more. Words create worlds because there are realities that flow around and under and through everything. What is most true and real about a thing is rarely simply the thing. Even writing about my old dining room table and calling out those aspects that it has been separated out for, made me immediately feel a sense of gratitude for the wood top and leggy thing. I had an emotional reaction to a table.

Naming things carefully creates order in our lives and opens doors for love and gratitude. Using words carelessly creates disorder and strife. The first thing we see God calling man to do in the garden is to name the animals. Oh, the glorious participation God calls his kids to. God invited Adam to separate out this animal from that and name it rightly.

If an emotional reaction was the result of properly separating out a dining room table, consider the impact of properly naming people. What is the effect of how I name myself? God named Himself to Moses on Mount Horeb at the burning bush. Moses asked God who He should tell the Pharoh sent him, and God responded, "I am who I am."

Dr. Michael LeFebvre wrote a wonderful essay for the Center for Hebraic Thought on the meaning of God's covenant name that He gave to Moses. Like Walton, he digs into some of the mindsets of the Jews in that day and the language that was used.

He wrote, "Confusion arises about the meaning of God's name translated "I am" and the related "Yahweh" when we read those terms through Western lenses. In English, for example, being verbs such as "am," "is," and "are" express either equivalence or existence...In many languages like English, the phrase "I am" indicates the speaker's existence. Read this way, the Lord's statement "I am" is a declaration, "I exist."

...In biblical Hebrew, the being verb hayah conveys not just existence but manifest existence. It indicates the appearance, presence, or standing of a thing... In the name Yahweh, God made himself known as a present being—present with and for his people. And wherever God's presence is invoked, that announcement is pregnant with the certainty of his attention, his care, his power, and his grace. Perhaps a helpful paraphrase of God's words at the burning bush would be, "Say to the people of Israel, 'I Am Present has sent me to you.'"[1]

It is easy for me to focus on God's naming of Himself in terms of His existence, or self-existence, or all-existence, and miss that His naming of Himself as I AM, was also ordering Himself in a very personal way. Do you see the glorious difference and the power of rightly naming? His name orders Himself positionally with me, as much as it describes His own greatness.

Scripture tells me that God has also named me. He tells me that my name is written in the Book of Life. Revelation 2 says that I will receive a white stone with a new name written on it. Isaiah 49 says that God has written the names of His people on His hands. But what name is it?

Do I suppose that the name written in the Book of Life is Aaron Porter? Of course not. My dad gave me that name, and no matter how many times he tried to tell me I was named after Moses' brother, I know that I was named after Elvis Aaron Presley (and don't tell me it wasn't spelled with two "As," he changed it!). The name I carry in this life is a temporary thing. I have another name. God gave me a name. I am dying to know what my real name is. For now, however, I have a lot of other voices trying to tell me my name.

Let us go back to the beginning of this chapter. "I'm ugly." "I'm an idiot." I am, I am, I am. The accuser names things as well. His names create disorder and bring shame, but they are so easy to believe. "I'm

---

1. Dr. Michael LeFebvre, February 15, 2022, *'I Am Who I am'? The Real Meaning of God's Name in Exodus,* <https://hebraicthought.org/meaning-of-gods-name-i-am-exodus/>

fat." Well, maybe I am overweight. "I'm a bad parent." Well, maybe I have been selfish and inattentive.

Names of accusation rely on material evidence, and since I have been taught to see reality through the lens of that which I experience with my senses, those names stick. If I only see names in those terms I will never be able to escape the clutches of condemnation. Naming myself rightly, or seeking to discover how God has named me separates me out, defines me, and gives me purpose. However, believing those names in the face of material evidence stacked against me requires faith.

I think of Jesus coming to Gideon while he was hiding in a winepress threshing wheat like a coward and calling him, "mighty warrior." I think of Jesus looking at Simon, the bombastic and unstable disciple, and naming him Peter, the rock. God's name for us could not be more opposite the "I am..." names that I give myself when I listen to the accuser.

As I begin to understand and claim the Gospel in a living and active way, I begin to learn my name and it reorders the chaos of my soul. Whenever I use or think the words "I am," or "I'm," I am about to reveal something about the condition of my heart. The "I am" statements I speak in my life will order or disorder my life. They will bring beautiful purpose or be purposed to keep me in shame. False "I am" statements have powerful purposes, they just hide in the shadows.

When I look at my own list of "I am" statements that spit in the face of the cross and turn my back on the love of my Father, I start to get a little angry. I start to feel something rise up in me that doesn't want to swallow those putrid declarations down like I have year after year after year. I start to reject it for the most beautiful reason. Not to fix me, not to do my work, but because of how it is so grossly offensive to my deepest love, the lover of my soul, my Savior, and my God

Have you ever heard a child, maybe your child, say awful things about themselves? I have heard my children declare themselves to be stupid when they struggled with school or ugly because someone made fun of them. I think I can say that it almost universally breaks our hearts to hear a beautiful little creature tear itself down. If that is my natural reaction, why would it not be my Heavenly Father's?

Learning to name things right, to order them through a gospel lens is a practice that God want's to be included in. It is something I get to build with God, instead of telling Him to go wait in the corner while I fix all my crap by myself. I find words that He has said first and I adopt as my own. I learn to use words that declare to my heart what He has already declared to me.

God reaches out in His love and whispers a script into my ear. "Hey kid...let's create something new. Let's reach into that disordered world you've spoken into being, the prisons that hold you in bondage, and let's build something new. It hurts me to see you live in that world. I love you so much. Trust me...this is going to be fun"

Then, in His still small voice, He roars, "Repeat after me, son."

In Christ I AM a new creature, the old has gone, behold the new has come (2 Cor. 5:17) I AM dead to sin and alive in Christ. (Romans 6:11) I AM not alone. (Hebrews 13:5) I AM set free, I AM not a slave. (Romans 8:2, John 8:32) I AM the precious little child of a perfect Father. (John 1:12) Oh the hours He would delight in that rebuilding work with you.

Don't misunderstand me. This is not the simple work of wielding Bible verses like some Harry Potter spell and everything bad just goes away. This is the work of taking our thoughts captive and carrying them chained to the Gospel and daily asking God, "Hey Dad, is this how you see me?" and then quieting our souls enough to hear the answer. Words create the worlds we live in, for better or for worse.

In the next chapters, we will seek to find gospelicious tools to help us rightly name ourselves and accept God's view of His precious kids. God's got two sets of tattoos. On his thigh, according to Revelation, it reads, King of Kings and Lord of Lords. That one is for the world to see. But on His hand, my name, my true name, always before His face.

Chapter Nine

Who Am I

To start to understand what God sees in regard to my identity, and to reckon the Gospel, I need to begin with the question, "Who am I?" That simple question has been debated in "modern" ways since the time of Plato. Philosophers have grappled with it, it has been tied into politics in determining what rights various individuals are afforded, and it lies at the base of ethics, epistemology, and metaphysics. Am I a dichotomy or a trichotomy? Am I a body, mind, and spirit, or is my spirit a part of my mind and there is just a physical and immaterial part of me? Bored yet? If you are not bored, by all means, read some of the material exhaustively written on the subject by incredibly smart folks.

Although I appreciate all of those deep thoughts and exhaustive answers, I need to keep it simpler so that I can make it practical. Who I am falls into two separate categories. The first, which is the thrust of this book, is what I call the "essential" or "eternal me." The second is the temporary me where the wrestling between flesh and spirit occurs and is the topic of Soul Architecture book 2.

What I mean by essential identity is, that which I am now that will continue to be me after I die. The me that endures. That part of me is born of the Spirit, sealed by the Spirit, and rests completely in the person and work of Christ. I'm sure you have heard the idiom, "too heavenly-minded to be of any earthly good." Understanding the difference between my eternal identity and my temporary helps me to avoid that trap.

The temporary parts of me will cease to be a part of my experience after I die. However, the eternal parts of me exist NOW, embodied in temporary parts, and will continue past the grave. That might seem like a simple thought but it unravels a whole lot of bad theology I was taught in my youth. The way eternal life was presented when I was younger was that eternal life began when I died and thus everything here on earth (other than winning souls to Christ) was just rearranging furniture on the Titanic.

When I recognize that my essential identity is in full play right now and will continue, then I realize that my eternal life has already begun. It's happening now. God's Kingdom is not just a thing that is yet to come but it is alive and active in the hearts of His people. How I engage my relationship with God and the world He put me in matters because it's all a part of my essential self, the eternal part of me.

The gnostics at the time of the early Church were trying to push the idea that everything in the body or the physical world was bad and that people needed to go inward and find secret knowledge or the divine spark within themselves. That is not what we are talking about. God created our bodies and the physical world and broken though it all is, there is beauty and worshipful interaction that occurs within that journey. But as we will see in the next couple of chapters, it is very easy to begin to confuse my identity, who I believe that I essentially am, with the temporary parts of my "self."

That is a hard trap to avoid because the temporary stuff is what I easily and naturally see. The essential part of me, my Gospel identity, requires faith in what God says that He sees.

In 1 Samuel 16, Samuel, the great prophet and last judge of Israel was rebuked by God for just this problem when he was sent to crown the second King of Israel. He thought that David's older brothers seemed much more like the kingly sorts than the scrawny little brother. He of all people should have known better. He had crowned the people's king, Saul. He was made king because he was super tall and hot. OK, I added the last part, but he was the kind of man other men wanted to be like and who made the women take a second glance. Now Samuel comes to crown another king for Israel and sees David's cooler hotter, OK I added that last part, older brother, and thinks, this must be the one. God answers him in verse 7, "Do not look on his appearance or on the height of his stature, because I have rejected him. For the Lord sees not as man sees: man looks on the outward appearance, but the Lord looks on the heart." The Lord does not see as man sees. We look at mirror reflections for identity, He sees something completely different and utterly surprising.

So how do I come to discern what is the essential me and what is the temporary? Here is my simplistic way of sussing it out from day to day.

The person I see reflected in the mirror is not the essential me. That person has changed since the day I was conceived. I am not the twelve-year-old who stared at the birthing of fresh pimples as he brushed his teeth in the morning before school. Nor will I be the man who is today deciding whether or not it is a shaving day. I will continue to wax and age, erode and decay until I die, and then I will be put in the ground, and this vessel I have seen in the mirror all my life will cease to hold...me. Therefore, what I see in the mirror cannot be essentially me, for I will still exist, but what I see in the mirror today will be food for the worms and a new body will be mine forever. This body I see is a temporary vehicle for this part of this journey. That does not make it unimportant, but there is something _more me_ that can't be reflected in the glass.

That one is simple, right? The physical me that I see is not the eternal part of me because it will die and stop being a part of my experience as... me.

I can take that obvious notion a step further. Throughout my life, I told myself and others who I was based on achievements, failures, or desires. I might believe that I AM (identity statement) a terrible and shameful person because of my sinful desires and actions. But isn't that also part of the temporary vehicle for me through which I discover God's love and grace? When I die won't those things also come to an end? Do you believe that your sinful desires and actions will go with you into glory? Will the struggles of the flesh accompany you to that side of the grave? I certainly hope not. That would be very disappointing if you arrived on the other side of death and your first desire was your favorite sin. In that day He will wipe away every tear, and I will know Him as I am known.

So if those sinful desires and broken stories, like my flesh, end when this part of my journey ends, then they are also not a part of my essential self. Again, those parts of me are not useless, they are purposeful and important. Do not discount or discredit the temporary. However, I have to put them in their proper place and not let the temporary eclipse the eternal, thus bringing my Gospel identity to nothing but a few stanzas in my favorite worship song. What I will practically experience is an identity built on past and present sins and struggles, and that is an identity that will never bring me to abundant life.

How sad that I cast off God's truth that I am dead to sin so easily. It is no longer my identity; I am a new creature in Christ. I no longer sin, but it is the sin that dwells in me that is the real culprit of my chaos and confusion (Rom. 7). I am united with Christ, clothed in Christ, reigning with Christ, victorious with Christ. Those are all things that exist now and that I will carry into eternity because of the person and work of Jesus. The parts of me that are the essential me are how God sees me, for He does not see as man sees. Because of that truth, I can claim with conviction that there is no condemnation for those that are in Christ.

The only way I will start to see myself as God sees me is to understand a little more clearly what God meant when He gave those wonderful promises listed in the paragraph above. I have to find tethers that will bind those words to my soul.

Chapter Ten

Tale of Two Adams

I remember when family tree websites started getting popular. I was all in. I paid extra to get European information and I was able to trace one line of my family back to the 1300s. Knowing where we come from matters. Knowing our family and heritage matters. I had a conversation with Wendell Moss, a therapist and educator out of the Allender Center that showed me reasons for that importance that surprised and excited me. I'll let you look him up so he can do his own talking on the subject, I wouldn't do it justice. An important part of knowing who we are is knowing where we come from, even if our family of origin makes us uncomfortable.

After the initial wave and lineage searching, I started watching videos of people who took it a step further. They began taking DNA tests. Most were completely surprised by the results. They found that they had a family lineage that stretched out to countries and people groups that they never expected to be connected to. Most of the time they didn't look much like people who came from those countries, but there it was, it was in their blood and every strand of their hair.

God gave us a way to understand our identities in a similar way. He tells us to take a spiritual DNA test and to check our results with the cross. First, let me dispel what I believe to be a widely accepted myth. God isn't trying to clean up sinners. That's not what salvation is. He isn't trying to simply fix them. He wants to kill them. Just slay them. Dead.

So, yes, I love provocative statements. They are fun. However, how is that as provocative as it seems? Here are some verses most of us have heard and many of us were asked to memorize in Sunday school or AWANAS. "I have been crucified with Christ, I no longer live..." (Gal. 2:20) "In Christ, I am a new creature, the old has gone, behold, the new has come" (2 Cor. 5:17). I have been killed, executed with Christ. The only reason that my statement that God wants to kill sinners would be provocative is if we turn all of these kinds of verses into metaphors.

Read this portion of Romans 6. Don't rush through it. "Do you not know that all of us who have been baptized into Christ Jesus were baptized into his death? We were buried therefore with him by baptism into death, in order that, just as Christ was raised from the dead by the glory of the Father, we too might walk in newness of life. For if we have been united with him in a death like his, we shall certainly be united with him in a resurrection like his. We know that our old self was crucified with him in order that the body of sin might be brought to nothing, so that we would no longer be enslaved to sin. For one who has died has been set free from sin. Now if we have died with Christ, we believe that we will also live with him. We know that Christ being raised from the dead will never die again; death no longer has dominion over him. For the death he died he died to sin, once for all, but the life he lives he lives to God. So you also must consider (reckon) yourselves dead to sin and alive to God in Christ Jesus. " (v. 3-11)

That entire passage screams out to us, not in metaphor, but in a spiritual reality that God wants to kill us...and then resurrect us. Only then do we have the hope of a new reality, DNA, a new identity.

We will talk more about the part of our identity that is connected to adoption in an upcoming chapter, but we are going to start here. Our adoption as children of God is more than any human adoption because it includes a DNA swap. The only way for me to change my human DNA would be for me to die and get myself reincarnated, born of someone else. Only then would I carry their DNA (unless I got a bone marrow transplant, but even then I would still carry my family's DNA). That is the simple, mysterious, and miraculous answer Jesus gave to Nicodemus when the Pharisee came seeking direction from the Lord in the dead of night:

"Now there was a man of the Pharisees named Nicodemus, a member of the Jewish ruling council. He came to Jesus at night and said, 'Rabbi, we know you are a teacher who has come from God. For no one could perform the miraculous signs you are doing if God were not with him.' In reply, Jesus declared, 'I tell you the truth, no one can see the kingdom of God unless he is born again.'" John 3:1-3

This interaction has become normalized for many Christians because the phrase "born again" (which Jesus coined that very night) became a popular part of many Christian's vocabulary. "Are you born again, brother?" The phrase "born again" became shortcut language for something deep and profound. When we accept shortcut language into our vernacular, it can slowly erode the depth of its meaning. After all, why would we need a shortcut for something that was simple to begin with? In this case, many folks' familiarity with the phrase has robbed this interaction between Jesus and Nicodemus of it's weirdness and how hard Jesus' words are to accept.

Do you know how I know that what Jesus said was totally weird? Nicodemus responded to that statement with a sarcastic answer. "Born again? I'm old. Am I supposed to wiggle myself back into my mum's womb? Just climb on back in there?"

Seriously? He came to Jesus because he claimed to have enough insight to know that Jesus was a teacher who had come from God. Jesus gives him a profound truth bomb. And then he gets sarcastic and snarky with the Son of God incarnate? That's both hilarious and terrifying. But as always, Jesus is so patient with the insolence of mankind. Just don't gloss over the weirdness. Being born again is not a normal thought, but it makes perfect sense when we couple that idea with others that God gives us to help us see what He sees concerning our identity.

Here is how God helps us understand this phenomenon that we cannot see with our physical eyes: "For just as through the disobedience of one man the many were made sinners, so also through the obedience of one man, the many will be made righteous. The law was added so that the trespass might increase. But where sin increased, grace increased all the more, so that, just as sin reigned in death, so also grace might reign through righteousness to bring eternal life through Jesus Christ our Lord. " (Rom. 5:19-21)

"Through the disobedience of one man, the many were made sinners." God is, of course, talking about Adam, the first man. Watchman Nee has a saying that I have always loved concerning this verse "I am not a sinner because I sin, but I sin because I come of the wrong stock. I sin because I am a sinner."[1] You are not a sinner because you sin; you sin because you are a sinner. In other words, you did not become a sinner the first time you told a lie to your parents or took that extra cookie from the cookie jar. Those actions only proved your

---

1. Nee, Watchman. Watchman Nee Special Collection : The Normal Christian Churck Life and The Normal Christian Life (p. 254). Kindle Edition.

family heritage, your fallen lineage, your sinful DNA. We were simply Adam's kids. Don't worry, the story doesn't end there. There is more than one Adam. There was that first Adam in the garden, but God also gave us the gift of a last Adam, a final Adam, Jesus.

"Thus it is written, 'The first man Adam became a living being'; the last Adam became a life-giving spirit." (1 Cor. 15:45) Yes, if you gave me a spiritual DNA test before I knew Jesus it would come back saying I was the child of Eden's Adam. No matter how hard I tried to look like the last Adam, my blood would reveal my real family. As we mentioned before, the only thing that can change my DNA would be to die and be reborn as someone else. Oh snap...that's what Jesus was trying to explain to Nicodemus.

Let me explain this through an odd example. Let's say that I really don't want to be a Porter. I'm sick of being a Porter. I want to get as far from being a Porter as I can get. I decide I want to be Hmong. I love the movie Grand Torino, I like how they did community, and the food looked good, I want to be Hmong. So I change my name to Chue Vang. I changed it on my social security card, I changed it on my license. I am now Chue Vang. What have I changed? I've changed...my name. The annoying thing is that no one treats me like a Hmong dude. So I start dressing in the traditional clothes of the Hmong. I even learn to speak Dananshan. I get the look and the language in order. What have I changed? I grow increasingly pissed off because people still don't see me as Hmong, they see a Euro-mutt white guy dressed in outfits that are strange to the Western eye and speaking a language they don't understand. Having enough of the prejudice I go to the great expense of having plastic surgery and changing everything about my appearance to look spot-on Hmong. Finally, people started seeing me as Chue Vang and treating me like a foreign man from Asia. What have I changed?

In the end, I've changed all of the mirror aspects of me. If you were to draw my blood, it would still say I'm a Porter. The truth of my lineage is in my blood. To be a Vang I would have to be born of a Vang. The truth is in the blood.

Now let's take this to churchianity. I can decide I want to be a Christian. I can change my membership card, get one that says that I took the classes, agreed to the tenants, and now I'm part of the club. I can start dressing like the people in my church and change my language to mimic the way they talk and the things they talk about. I can transform everything about myself so that no one would ever doubt that I'm one of them. But what have I changed? If you drew my blood it would either be the blood of the first Adam or the last Adam. The fact of who I am is in the blood, and it was blood that was offered to make it so. The proof and verification is in the blood.

I was crucified with Christ. The old man was put to death. But I was not left in such a state, I was resurrected with Christ, I was born again, made into a new creature. When God sees me with those eyes that are not like man's eyes, He sees a DNA that I cannot see. He sees the Holy and beautiful DNA of His beloved Son. 2 Corinthians 5:21 says, "For our sake he made him to be sin who knew no sin, so that in him we might become the righteousness of God." Sometimes I behave righteously and sometimes I fail to. However, in Christ, I have BECOME the righteousness of God. My total being is the righteousness of Christ. It's a fact of my DNA. That is the tale of two Adams. That is why I must be born again.

In the last chapter, we talked about our essential identity, our eternal self that is now and will be beyond the grave. This is my essential self. All that is hidden in Christ and sealed by the Spirit. In the chapter before that, we talked about being very careful about what words we use to declare our identity. This is the identity that must remain clear with every one of those declarations. But still, there is a problem.

Chapter Eleven

But I Am Not Who God Says I Am

The fact that we can't see my miraculous death and resurrection physically can make my "new creature" status hard to believe. However, when I keep craving and doing the same things from before the transformation, it can feel impossible to trust. In our worst moments of self-condemnation, we all must face the question, How real can this Gospel be if I still think and do these things? Worse, what if I believed it and did OK for a while and then utterly crashed and burned?

To face that question without merely throwing back half-hearted Christian platitudes takes true Gospel reckoning. It requires a belief that has penetrated deeper than intellectual assent to a principle body of dogmas. Paul is a great example of a reckoned human. He faced the same problem of his flesh that we all do and did so without mincing words.

"I do not understand what I do. For what I want to do I do not do, but what I hate I do. And if I do what I do not want to do, I agree that the law is good. As it is, it is no longer I myself who do it, but it is sin living in me. I know that nothing good lives in me, that is, in my sinful nature. For I have the desire to do what is good, but I cannot carry it out. For what I do is not the good I want to do; no, the evil I do not want to do-- this I keep on doing. Now if I do what I do not want to do, it is no longer I who do it, but it is sin living in me that does it. " (Rom. 7:15-20)

Without placing a Gospel template over that paragraph, it is the biggest copout in the history of sacred writings. "I don't know...I keep doing the stuff I don't want to do, you know, sin, but it's not really me, it's the bad stuff that lives in me that does it." Excuse me? Honestly, if any of my children said that to me after the fifth time they broke a rule, I would take issue with the child. I would react in a way that was far from gracious and I would probably feel bad about myself as a parent afterward. In other words, no kid of mine better quote Paul when they screw up.

But step back for a moment and put this amazing paragraph into the context of the two DNAs, the two Adams. Paul is standing firmly in an identity that he actually believes exists.

Here's how it breaks down for him. Yes, he lives in a vehicle that is of the flesh. It is not the essential "him" because it will be dead and separated from his experience of existence eventually. His flesh vehicle craves flesh fuel. It is not surprising but it is frustrating. But, if he does what he does not want to do in the Spirit - in his Gospel identity - then it is not the real Paul who is doing it, but that flesh vehicle that he's cohabiting with until it breathes its last.

It's kind of like this: I once owned a dog that I particularly liked. His name was Roscoe. He was a big muscular cross between a Rhodesian Ridgeback and a Staffordshire Bull Terrier. Besides his constant barking problem and the digging-up-the-grass-to-pursue-gophers problem, he had one flaw that perpetuated his eventual exit from the family. Roscoe hated blondes.

When I say that Roscoe hated blondes, I don't mean that he preferred redheads. If he saw a blonde woman, he would go completely insane. Mind you, this was a big scary scary-looking dog. He would literally bite at his fence and try to pull it down when he saw blond women. Clearly, this rescue dog had some blonde trauma in his past. Unfortunately, there was a blonde girl who was relatively new to the youth group I was pastoring at the time who was quite certain that she could change my dog's mind. It turns out, she could not. She put her hand through the fence to make friends and Roscoe gladly accepted the treat.

So after Roscoe had his fill of blonde flesh, I met the young lady's mother for the first time. Information was exchanged, money was offered to pay for any medical expenses, and I came to a critical conclusion: I did not bite the blonde girl.

You thought I was going somewhere else with that, didn't you? It may be obvious, but it's true. I didn't hate blonde women. I did not feel violent compulsions when I saw them. I did not bite the girl. I owned a dog that bit blonde women. I am not the dog.

There were consequences I had to bear because of my dog's behavior. I had responsibilities as the dog's owner. I needed a good fence to keep the dog from killing people. Hey, I'm not saying, nor is Paul, that we have no responsibility when it comes to our behavior or us acting out of our flesh cravings. There are both responsibilities and consequences when it comes to the sin we participate in, in our flesh.

However, the responsibility and consequences for my dog are very different from my identity as the dog. I did not sit around for days after the blonde girl incident wondering when I became such a strange and twisted man, that I would bite a high school girl's hand and draw blood. Ridiculous. It was clear that the dog was the dog and I was me.

In Romans 7, Paul is having that same conversation. He is speaking with crystal clarity concerning the flesh for which he takes responsibility and the life from which he draws an identity. Until we "count," "reckon," "come to grips with," or "reconcile ourselves to" a Gospel identity, there is nothing religion can do to help us. Christ is of no value, for Christ is not resurrected in our lives; He is not living. He is nothing more than an idea onto which we add the accessories of religiosity and the social community of the so-called "church."

In Christ, you are a new creature. Either it is so, or it is not. It is not a premise that is in daily flux, nor a supposition based on your works. It is a fact of birth. You did nothing to gain the DNA of the first Adam, nor can your re-birthed DNA come and go based on your behavior. You are who God has declared you to be. Living it is the trick.

I grew up listening to stories on records as I played with Star Wars action figures in my room. One I particularly loved was the story of the Prince and the Pauper. In the story, the prince meets a beggar who looks exactly like him and they trade places. The prince discovers the pain and misery of living outside of the palace walls. Friends, he was still the prince. I am still a co-heir with Christ, a prince, even when I am digging for moldy scraps of food in the dumpster of my life. My EXPERIENCE is not princely, but I am still the son of a King who is beckoning me back to His table.

You are who God says you are. Now we get to go through the sanctification process through which we experience that reality more and more in this temporary flesh vehicle. Book 2 of Soul Architecture deals specifically with that journey. In that book, we will spend our time fleshing out our flesh and our temporary but important experience with it. For now, please remember, we are focussing on that part of ourselves that exists now and will continue beyond the grave. Within that identity, we find the power to discover joy in God's love and the adventure of muddling through the confusing mess and beauty of the world we live in now.

Chapter Twelve

The Deal Was Not Yours

Honestly, I am no less confused by my own heart than Paul seemed to be about his. I see these words, written down in the Scriptures, words that I believe are from God's own heart, but do I live like I believe they mean any of what they say?

It's as if vicious enemies surround me, thoughts and doubts that attack my identity and seek to drag me back to believing that my flesh is me. But then God scoops me up and draws a circle in the dirt, tucking me beneath Him, clenching his cinder block fists, and dares anyone to cross the line and take His child. And still, I try to crawl out...I crawl out.

I've always had a picture in my mind of a courtroom. I sit with Jesus at the defendant's table. I look across at the prosecutor, the accuser. He rises and lays his case before the judge, God enthroned before us. His case is really strong. He has exhibit after exhibit of evidence that shows exactly who I am, exactly how I have failed. I am transfixed. He is so damn eloquent.

Soon I find myself getting up and slinking over to his table. I catch a little grin pull up at the corner of the prosecutor's mouth as I do. Jesus sees it too but He doesn't try to stop me. The one who stands in intercession for me waits for his turn. When the accuser finishes, He takes His place before the judge. I see a slight smile pull up at the judge's mouth as well as He looks at His son and nods for him to commence. Jesus doesn't need words. He simply and slowly pulls his sleeves up His arms and holds them forth. One exhibit, one piece of evidence. Scars. Without a word, he pulls His sleeves back down and comes to me where I sit next to the accuser. He reaches down and gently takes my hand and we walk from the courtroom without a backward glance.

He has never lost a case.

To begin to walk with any confidence in our Gospel identities, we must learn to see through God's lens. For far too long, most of us have looked through lenses of accusation and self-condemnation. These are the tools of Satan, for it is he who is called the "Accuser of the brethren" (Rev. 12:10). Satan wants me to look in the mirror and believe that what I see is my identity. Christ calls me in and through the looking glass, to see what lies on the other side:

"What then shall we say to these things? If God is for us, who can be against us? He who did not spare his own Son but gave him up for us all, how will he not also with him graciously give us all things? Who shall bring any charge against God's elect? It is God who justifies. Who is to condemn? Christ Jesus is one who died — more than that, who was raised — who is at the right hand of God, who indeed is interceding for us. Who shall separate us from the love of Christ? Shall tribulation, or distress, or persecution, or famine, or nakedness, or danger, or sword? As it is written, "For your sake we are being killed all the day long; we are regarded as sheep to be slaughtered." No, in all these things we are more than conquerors through him who loved us. For I am sure that neither death nor life, nor angels nor rulers, nor things present nor things to come, nor powers, nor height nor depth, nor anything else in all creation, will be able to separate us from the love of God in Christ Jesus our Lord." (Romans 8:31-39)

Understanding where I anchor my identity is not that hard to discern. If another Christian were to walk up to me and say, "So...how are things going?" how would I answer? And what reason would I give for the answer?

I might say, "I'm doing great. Just came back from time away with God. I had a lot of time in His word. Did my devotionals every day this week."

Or I might say, "Not doing so well, drank too much last weekend. Kind of struggling."

Or maybe I'd say, "Doing awesome; prayer times have been lovely."

Maybe I'd say, "I lost my temper with my kid and yelled at them. I'm such a bad person."

Don't get me wrong. Intimate times with God ought to feel good; sin should prick the conscience and feel uncomfortable. But, honestly, that's not usually what we mean when we say those kinds of things. My identity, the way I see myself as a Christian, is always dangerously and precariously balanced on the precipice of performance. If I perform well, I feel good ABOUT myself. If I perform poorly, I feel bad ABOUT myself.

When I am approaching my identity like that, Christ's invitation to die with Him and become reborn in His resurrection has very few, if any, practical implications in my life. In the beginning, those were the things I trusted to get me saved, but everything else was on me and based on my performance. I was looking for something tangible to base my identity feelings on. Religious ideas and stained-glass-word pictures did not give enough assurance to keep me going when self-doubt and shame destroyed my fragile "equilibrium."

So what's the problem?

Roman 3:23-25 says, "...all have sinned and fall short of the glory of God, and are justified freely by his grace through the redemption that came by Christ Jesus. God presented him as a sacrifice of atonement, through faith in his blood. He did this to demonstrate his justice, because in his forbearance he had left the sins committed beforehand unpunished."

In our sterile society, where we buy packaged meat at the store and rarely see blood, the blood of Jesus is a hard thing to grasp. Yet God says, "We have now been justified by his blood, how much more shall we be saved from God's wrath through him!" (Rom. 5:9)

The only thing that can make us feel better about our situation in life is Christ's blood. A deal was struck before the foundation of the world. God the Father and God the Son said, "Okay," and the deal went down. I would not impugn God's character by explaining it beyond that, but it went down. And Jesus went to the cross, and at the cross, He cried out Tetelestai…"Debt paid in full. It is finished."

Our great struggle is that we think we are supposed to feel something of this "blood of Jesus." The deal was set between the Father and the Son; the Son accomplished it before the Father. It is not ours to have an opinion about. The efficacy of the blood of Christ is for God to value, and ours to stand in awe of and to trust. Believe it or don't believe it, but how one feels about it has nothing to do with it.

I have an adopted son. Long before he ever knew I was coming for him, I worked on his behalf. I paid fees and jumped through legal hoops. My love was being lavished on him before I ever held him in my arms or smelled his baby head (am I the only one who adores baby heads?). An agency set the price, and I and others sacrificed and paid it. It was my honor, my choice to do so.

I cannot imagine a time in my son's life when he looks at me and says, "I am not your son. The price you paid was not enough to cover the bill." Ridiculous! It's already done. He was the beneficiary of all that I described but the deal was not between me and him. The price and the payment were done apart from him

Every adopted child faces some crisis of identity and we, the adopted children of God, are no exception. But may our identity struggles never be over the price of our adoption.

"This is the message we have heard from him and declare to you: God is light; in him there is no darkness at all. If we claim to have fellowship with him yet walk in the darkness, we lie and do not live by the truth. But if we walk in the light, as he is in the light, we have fellowship with one another, and the blood of Jesus, his Son, purifies us from every sin." (I Jn 1:5-7)

I grew up singing hymns. The blood of Christ came up in those songs more than it seems to these days, but it still comes up. As I started considering how much the blood was not an idea or metaphor, but was a physical tangible payment for my adoption, it changed all of those lyrics that had lay dormant in my heart.

It's OK for me to tell God, I don't get this. I don't understand why you chose blood. I don't know why Jesus had to go through all that He did to pay for me. I don't like it. It breaks my heart. But Dad, I believe that You see it differently than me. I believe that You value it differently than me. Help me believe that it is enough for you to love me the way you say that you do.

As we move into our new identity in Christ, we remain firmly planted, despite our struggles with this vehicle of flesh in which we reside, because the blood of Christ has actual value to our Father. It is not merely an idea to Him. It is an accomplished purpose. It is finished.

Chapter Thirteen

Re-Created In My Image

When we stumble and fail, what is it that pulls us back up? What cleanses our conscience and sets us back into Kingdom life? "The blood of goats and bulls and the ashes of a heifer sprinkled on those who are ceremonially unclean sanctify them so that they are outwardly clean. How much more, then, will the blood of Christ, who through the eternal Spirit offered himself unblemished to God, cleanse our consciences from acts that lead to death, so that we may serve the living God!" (Heb. 9:13-14)

Our identity rests on the solid substance of Christ's blood, and a covenant struck between God and man, with both sides of the covenant physically fulfilled by persons of the Triune God. God wants you to know:

"For you know that it was not with perishable things such as silver or gold that you were redeemed from the empty way of life handed down to you from your forefathers, but with the precious blood of Christ, a lamb without blemish or defect." (1 Peter 1:18-19)

As we engage this journey at a personal level, each step must point back to this fact. All accusations and condemnations are lies that are not of God. For He has done exactly what He set out to do in His own requirements – perform a miraculous transformation in my life. I was spiritually crucified and resurrected with Christ through faith in His blood. And because of that, I am now and forever clothed in the righteousness of the Last Adam.

That said...Houston, we have a problem. Remember at the beginning of this book when we discussed how important it was to see God as a person, or an emotion-bearing entity? I'm not taking that back. However, I promised to expand on an innate danger that lurks in the shadow of that process.

The writer and philosopher Voltaire once said, "God created man in his image and man has returned to him the favor." At first glance, the witty sentiment from a man who did not believe in any kind of personal relationship between God and man looks like just another jab at Christians. But look again. Old Voltaire gave us a profound and essential truth.

When I am struggling with sin and shame, it is far easier to make God into a version of me in my mind than to accept the version that Scripture gives. Grace is fun to talk about until we need to accept it, then we would usually rather take a beating. Thus Voltaire's concept pushes me into hiding from God's love and away from the grace that is offered. Here is how it used to look for me:

When I was younger, I was a passive-aggressive manipulator. If someone hurt me, I would make sure they paid, but I would make them pay while still taking credit for being gracious. "It's OK," I would say with pain in my eyes, "I forgive you." Then I would withdraw for some alone time and make them feel my conspicuous absence, always making sure that they knew they had produced it.

It was a game. I wanted to see how far people would go to prove they loved me. Unfortunately, that adolescent behavior leaked into my theology. Other people play different games. Some are overtly aggressive. Some manipulate with tantrums and tears. Each behavior leaks into God's image a little differently.

If I offended God, I figured He must feel like I did, hurt and angry. I pictured that He needed some alone time. "It's fine Aaron; I forgive you. I just need a little space right now." Off He would go into some corner of heaven to sit behind a closed door and make me pay with His silence.

The picture in my head was being played at a mostly unconscious level. My response, however, was not. I would walk away in shame, believing God didn't want me around. I would wallow for a while. I would roll around in my humiliation like a pig luxuriating in its own excrement until I believed I had suffered enough to earn my way back into His love and affection, or enough time had passed that He could tolerate me again and overlook my wrongs.

The sad reality was that my picture of God's behavior had nothing to do with what I believed about God. I thought one thing and responded to him in a completely different way. The first problem with my response toward God was that it was predicated on God's surprise at my behavior. It was as if He was standing at the railing of heaven watching me move toward sin saying, "No, don't do it, Aaron." He covered His eyes with His hands but peeked between His fingers as I sinned. "Ahhh come on!" He'd burst out, slapping a hand down.

What a stupid thought. As if I have ever snuck up on God. But if I remove my ability to surprise God with my bad behavior, how can I retain the story that He is shocked and angry? Even in my life, I could usually maintain a very gracious response when others sinned toward me if I knew it was coming ahead of time. It's the surprise that gets me into trouble. As a parent I always have a gnawing feeling in the back of my mind that one of my kids might break my heart today, I just don't know when or how. But it is not so with God. This is what it means to believe one thing about God but live completely contrary to that belief.

Scripture paints an unambiguous picture of God's response toward foolish man. It starts in the Garden. God had made the "Book of Life of the Lamb that was slain before the foundations of the earth." Therefore, He knew that humankind would fail and was not surprised.

However, if there was ever a time for God to get really, really, really mad at sin, it was in the garden. He gave man one rule, and it wasn't even a hard rule: Don't eat a piece of fruit from a particular tree. It wasn't as if He set up an algebraic equation that Adam and Eve had to solve each day to stay in the garden. Just don't eat that fruit. That's it. This is called setting the bar extremely low.

Low bars, high bars, it doesn't matter. Man was created to find God through His sacrifice on the creature's behalf. Man failed the test, and it is here that we must pay close attention to God's reaction to man's failure.

Immediately, Adam and Eve felt shame, and they hid from God. Friend, there are many absurd aspects to this story, but each has an important purpose. Adam and Eve hiding in the bushes from God is absurdity number one. What did they think would happen? Did they believe God would lose at this game of hide-and-seek? I can't make too much fun of them for truth be told, they were as stupid as I am in my sin.

Part two: God comes after them. Take note, who is running from whom here? Is it not man that runs from God when they are in sin and shame? Though the story we may tell ourselves is that God doesn't want us around, or that He is angry or disappointed, the truth is that we are always the ones doing the running. God is ever walking toward His children, even in the moments of their failure.

God asked two questions: "Where are you?" That seems like a strange question. I grew up with Superman and I know how X-ray vision works. Surely God has something like that. His first question is a setup to the second. "Did you eat of the tree I told you not to eat from?" Another seemingly crazy question. God absolutely knew. What is he doing? Is He like a cat toying with the mouse He has is cornered?

Listen, friend. Whenever God does something that seems to make no sense, there is something really fun going on. These questions are beautiful, gracious, and kind. He is giving mankind our first opportunity for confession. The die was cast and the fruit had been eaten, but relationships still needed to be restored. God knew what they had done, but they needed to say it, to confess it. I have often wondered what the scene would have looked like if Adam and Eve had burst forth from the bushes with their pathetic leafy coverings and said, "Yes! We did it. We ate of the tree. We are so sorry. Forgive us."

Alas, they did not. Adam blamed Eve and the God who gave her to him. Eve blamed the serpent. Once again, if I were God, things would have gone very differently, thank goodness I'm not God. Instead of rolling His eyes at their really poor responses to His questions, God deals with their accusations. He deals with the serpent, He deals with the woman, and He deals with the man. Then in an extraordinary move, He makes them clothes, coverings from the skin of an animal. He kills the first living creature to cover their shame. Even in their worst moment, He shows that death will be the price for their sin, but He will sacrifice something else on their behalf.

This is the first story in Scripture regarding God's response to sinful man. Jesus repeats it in Luke when He tells the story of the Prodigal Son and gives the Pharisees a picture of His Father.

When we allow ourselves the space to reinterpret God's character based on our manipulative behavior and emotions, we rob ourselves of the grace that could be ours. We are made in God's image but God is not like us. He calls us to see Him for who He is and to respond to that person. He calls us to boldly approach the throne of grace, right at our time of need and find out just exactly how wonderful He is.

Chapter Fourteen

The Love the Father Has Given Us

Did you know that "Father" was Jesus' favorite name for God? I find His choice of terms to be very important and profoundly special. We are, after all, being transformed into His image, and we are told that His Spirit dwells within us. It is only natural then, that we should pay attention to the vocabulary of the One we are becoming like.

Here's a fact that is particularly, beautifully weird. The idea of God as an individual's personal father was not a very Jewish way of thinking in Jesus' day. Throughout the Old Testament, we find that God is referred to, or refers to Himself, as the father of the nation of Israel. Like so many other expressions of God's personality at that time, "father" was used in reference to His special people as a group. But now, when Jesus comes into the picture, the fullness of God in human form, something shifts for us, something deeply personal.

Let me be clear. I'm not saying that God changed or became different in any way with the advent of the Christ. What I am saying is that our outlook and perception were given a new angle and breadth. And I can't help but wonder how much joyful anticipation God Himself must have felt as that shift approached.

With the coming of the New Covenant, a fresh thread of language emerges. That thread leads us to what we will call, "Abba Theology." Our core belief in God as Father.

1 John 3:1 says, "See what kind of love the Father has given to us, that we should be called children of God; and so we are."

I grew up in the late 70s, and early 80s, listening to children's praise songs on vinyl, so when I hear this verse I immediately start to sing it in a round in my mind. Some of you who listened to Psalty the singing songbook will know what I'm talking about. The song used the translation, "Behold what manner of love the Father has given unto us, (clap, clap) that we should be called the sons of God." I like and dislike that translation for a few reasons.

I like the word, "behold." There is a big difference in my heart and head between the phrases, see what kind of love, and behold, what kind of love. We could get into the nuances of the Greek word and try to make a case for beholding something to mean, leaning toward something, perceiving it, taking it in as a whole, coming to an understanding of it, seeing something simply, taking it in visually. Whatever. When I say I like the word "behold" better, I simply mean that. No one uses the word "behold," unless there is something really good at the other end of that sentence. If you oversell something with the word, "behold," you are going to get caught. "Come in the living room everyone, quickly. BEHOLD, Taco Bell for all." Meh. Behold demands that the subject of the beholding is behold-worthy.

The statement in 1 John 3 is absolutely behold-worthy. Step back! The curtain is opening on an amazing thing! Behold the kind of love the Father is giving you. See it in awe. He is calling you his child! Behold it! Wonder at it! Let the emotion of it fill you until you are overwhelmed and undone.

So, yeah, I prefer "behold" on that one.

The other important bit is the Greek word for children that is used here. This word will come up again and again in later chapters, but for now, we need to see how it is attached to us as the kind of love the Father has given to us. The word is teknon. It is a gender-neutral word, not son or daughter, describing those who are dependent. It is a tender word as much as a technical one. When I read through the New Testament passages where teknon is used, and I allow myself to feel the compassionate intimacy that is attached to it, over and over those verses become more rich and meaningful. It is the word that a parent uses for a precious little dependent child.

Behold the kind of love the Father is giving to you, that you should be called his precious little child, and so you are.

That is what this book is about. Stop, behold, and let the transformative truth of God's paternal love take your breath away. However, the journey only begins at the beholding. It must continue to the sacred grove where we experientially claim the truth for ourselves. If we fail to take that journey, we become romanticized Christians filled with pretty Christian notions and inspiring ideas that will lack real-life change, with no real-life experience to prove that these truths produce anything more than mere good feelings.

"But to all who did receive him, who believed in his name, he gave the right to become children of God." John 1:12

Pause. Take a deep breath. Go back and read that verse again slowly.

Do you see it? We have been given the right, the authority, to be called children of God.

Rights can be tricky things. As bondservants of Christ, we are called to lay down our rights, take up our crosses, and follow Jesus. We are given other rights by our government and we hold tenaciously to them, but by what right do we claim those rights?

The founding fathers said that they are self-evident, that we have been endowed by our creator with certain unalienable rights. Please understand, I like my rights to life, liberty, and the pursuit of happiness, but at various eras throughout history, that statement would have been laughable. If I were an indentured servant at the time of Christ, I would have had very limited rights. If the Romans decided my country sat on a piece of land they wanted, they would not have been gracious about respecting my self-evident rights.

I only bring that up to point out how extraordinary this declaration was at the time it was declared. We were given THE RIGHT to be called his teknon. If it is my right, then no man can take it from me. Neither my flesh nor my shame can rob me of it. Oh, that I would cling to that right with as much passion as I do my rights to life, liberty, and the pursuit of happiness. Oh, that I would join in protest of any group, sacred or secular, that would try to rob me of it.

Further, the authority or governing body that confers a right also has the duty to protect it. We see that in our experience as citizens. If someone tries to take something from me that the law has given me a right to, it is the government that is supposed to step in and protect that right. It is an insanely big thought to consider that God has given me that right and He is the authority who will protect it in the face of anyone who tries to take it away from me.

Sadly, as with any other right, I can choose to live in a way that keeps me from experiencing it. I might have the right to a piece of property, for example, but if I never claimed it and chose to live in a box on the sidewalk instead, my property would sit abandoned.

All rights must be claimed to be enjoyed, but my failure to claim a right does not nullify the fact that it is still mine. The absolute nature of this right does not require me to claim it in order for God to recognize it and act accordingly. However, my failure to claim it will drastically diminish my experience during the short decades of my journey through this life.

This right was not free. I'm sure you've heard someone say that God's love is unconditional. That statement is both correct and dangerously inaccurate. God's love and my right to be called His child is unconditional in that it is not dependent on anything I have done or will do. However, it is dependent on the person and sacrifice of Jesus, which is no small condition. Throughout the rest of this book, we have to remember everything we discussed at the beginning. My new identity is intact because of the person and work of Jesus and now that new identity gives me confidence to press into my new relationship with my Abba.

I spent a number of years conducting a random survey of strangers that I chanced upon throughout my day. While standing in line at a coffee shop or the grocery store, I would ask someone nearby, whether they were young or old, "Hey, please fill in the blank, Jesus died on the cross for my…" Without fail, their answer would be, "Sins." (I know, that's what most of you thought too.) Now, pause for a moment to consider that answer. Why is that the automatic response? Why is it so deeply ingrained?

The answer seems to revolve around our obsession with sin and sin management. Can you think of anything else Jesus died on the cross for? Take a moment. Did Jesus' death on the cross complete or fulfill anything besides forgiveness of sin?

Jesus did die on the cross to pay the price for my sins. But according to Scripture, He also died on the cross to bring me new life. He died on the cross to make me a new creature. He died on the cross to bring me into a relationship with His Father. He died on the cross to cleanse my conscience. The list of accomplishments goes on and on, but during the two or three years I was asking that question, not one single person said anything except, "Jesus died on the cross for my sins."

I don't say this to shame us. We were taught to think this way, and the concept matched up with our shame and the voice of the accuser that rings so loudly in our ears. But what if we listen to the voice of our Daddy? What does He say? What does the Spirit cry out within me?

Friend, precious friend, sin is not the main character in your story. Sin is not the yin to God's yang. Neither sin nor Satan is God's archrival. In Jesus, God's victory is COMPLETE. Sin is a plot point in your life, not a main character. Sin breaks us, shatters our pretensions, and drives us to the glorious grace we have in Christ. Sin teaches us our desperate need for rescue and leaves us with no hope but Jesus. In Jesus, sin has already been defeated, period. Add anything to that and we remove the Gospel. Jesus dying on the cross for my sins is vital, but that vital truth leads us to other truths and hopes. If I constantly go back to sin as my primary focus then I am in danger of experiencing death with Jesus but not a resurrection with Him.

I am clothed in the righteousness of Christ. I have become the righteousness of God through Jesus. I am dead to sin and alive in Christ. Nothing can separate me from my Father's love.

Let's be honest. The problem is that grace doesn't make any sense. My natural inclination, therefore, is to dilute grace in order to make it palatable. Decades ago I heard a speaker at a youth camp (sorry for not remembering your name buddy) explain grace something like this:

Let's pretend I go out driving. I have a hankering for speed, so I take off through town, convertible top down and the wind in my hair, blasting through stop-lights and weaving through traffic, 65...70...80...90 miles per hour. Buildings streak by as the sound of car horns trails behind me like the tail of a comet. At 100 miles per hour, I let out a whoop of exultation.

Not long after the needle crosses 120 I hear a siren behind me, and a motorcycle closes in, lights on. I pull over, a sick feeling in the pit of my stomach. I know what I've done and I do not doubt that there will be a price to pay.

The officer dismounts and, hand on his gun, approaches the apparent lunatic who just drove 120 miles per hour through town. He reaches the window and asks for my license and registration. I hand it over, and the officer informs me that, although I should be arrested for my reckless behavior, he is just going to give me a ticket. Whew! Thank God for small mercies.

The officer fills out the ticket and hands it to me. I scan the ticket for the fine. It's $3,000! My stomach lurches again. I don't have $3,000. What am I supposed to do with this? I can't pay. I watch as the officer returns to his bike, but halfway back he stops and turns around.

Dammit, dammit, dammit. Did he change his mind? What is happening? And how could I have been so stupid?

I roll down my window a second time. The officer looks at me for a moment. He reaches inside my car and takes the ticket back. As I watch, he slowly rips it up, piece...by...piece. "Now go," he says and turns back to his motorcycle.

I'm stunned. What just happened? Why in the world would he do that? Was it grace? No, that was not grace. It was mercy. I did not get what I deserved. I received mercy.

I turn the ignition and, just as I put the car in gear, I check the review mirror again to see the officer walking back in my direction. "Hold it," he says. As he approaches I roll down my window for the third time. Now there is a different expression on the officer's face, one I can't quite place. He reaches into a pocket, withdraws a checkbook, and begins writing. When he's finished, he tears the check from the pad, hands it to me, and walks away.

As the officer pulls back onto the road and drives off, I look at the check. His check. His personal check, and find that it is written to me for the sum of $3,000.

The end.

My first thought when I heard that story was that that was the dumbest story I had heard in a long time. That would never happen. I think in the history of traffic stops this has never happened. Mercy is believable. Not getting what I deserve is believable. But grace? Getting what I do NOT deserve? When we put it in stories attached to real life, it is absurd. The story is preposterous, even though it involves the relatively paltry sum of $3,000. Sure, I'd love a check for $3,000, but that's hardly winning the lottery.

However, when the Bible says in Ephesians 2, " For by grace you have been saved through faith. And this is not your own doing; it is the gift of God, not a result of works, so that no one may boast," it is describing an even more unfathomable gift. The means by which I was made righteous, made holy because Jesus was enough, was grace. More than merely the withholding of a punishment, it was a check handed to a felon. If a gift of $3,000 feels ridiculous to you, let me assure you that truly accepting the magnitude of God's grace will require a lot of work for all of us. You will not FEEL it automatically, because it's too big and unlikely. And yet it is yours just the same.

That said, just like our rights, a check is only a piece of paper until you cash it. And the cash does not make any difference until you spend it.

Let us pity the Christian who is still holding the check of God's grace, who framed it and mounted it on the wall, who tells the story of that wonderful day on the side of the road when they received it, but never spent a dime of it. Let us mourn for the Christian who still insists on living by credit and going deeper into the debt of shame and guilt while the check sits right there. My dear brothers and sisters, we need to learn to spend it, all of it.

I have a subscription to a company that makes computer programs for music production. I downloaded what I needed years ago and hadn't gone back to the site. A few days ago a friend of mine told me about some new programs on the site. I logged on the next morning and I was like a kid in a candy store. I couldn't afford most of what I saw, but I had the subscription. I clicked and downloaded for hours, filled with childish delight. I downloaded things I knew I would rarely use. I was reckless in my purchases because it had already been paid for. Oh that I would learn to be reckless in daily spending the treasure of the grace that I have been given, and feel the joy of the purchase of big and small things in my life that fills me with gratitude and spiritual delight.

This can sound scary as if that kind of grace will lead to sinful behavior unchecked. Grace is not a license to indulge the flesh, as Paul reminds the Romans, but an invitation to abundant life.

Further, for me to not spend the grace that has been given to me is an act of arrogant defiance against the Gospel. If I sin and choose to pay for it myself through shameful wallowing or more sin management it is either me saying that I don't believe that the blood of Christ was enough to deal with it or it is me saying that I would rather go in debt to religiosity than let God love me in the manner He asked to. Accepting God's grace in our time of need requires a great amount of humility when I am not using it as a license to sin.

Please don't fall into the trap of believing that spending the grace that has been given to us is only related to our sin or flesh. I want to spend it every time I pray so that there is nothing between me and my

Dad. I want to spend it every time I interact with my children so that I see them as God does. I want to spend it as I walk around the city I live in and come in contact with other children of God, made in his image, who have needs and pains of their own.

There is absolutely nothing stopping you, now that you have received grace. Sin has been defeated and nothing is keeping you from making today and tomorrow and the next day a sacred journey, full of joy and hope and purposeful suffering. Sin is now just a plot point that brings you back to the wellspring of His grace, where you will always find love and refreshment. It is by grace that you have become what you are, who you are. It is finished.

Behold the kind of love God has given to you, that you should become the precious little child of God. In Christ, it is your right.

So go now. But stop driving 100 miles per hour through town. That's just stupid.

Chapter Fifteen

Adoption

We talked a little bit about adoption earlier, but let's expand on it. Remember, this love the Father has given to us is a right that is rooted in a covenant that requires a process and payment. God's love is not simply an idea. It has been demonstrated in a process ordained before time began, a legal adoption.

"For all who are led by the Spirit of God are sons of God. For you did not receive the spirit of slavery to fall back into fear, but you have received the Spirit of adoption as sons, by whom we cry, 'Abba! Father!' The Spirit himself bears witness with our spirit that we are children of God, and if children, then heirs—heirs of God and fellow heirs with Christ, provided we suffer with him in order that we may also be glorified with him." Romans 8:14-17

Ephesians 1:4-5 tells us we were chosen, that He always knew he would adopt us. It tells us that we are His beloved and recipients of his grace.

Galatians 4:3-5 says, "When we were children, we were enslaved to the elementary principles of the world. But when the fullness of time had come, God sent forth his Son, born of woman, born under the law, to redeem those who were under the law, so that we might receive adoption as sons. And because you are sons, God has sent the Spirit of his Son into our hearts, crying, 'Abba! Father!' So you are no longer a slave, but a son, and if a son, then an heir through God."

The Greek word for adoption in those passages is a compound verb that literally means to make someone a son. It is important to understand that the concept of adoption in the Jewish culture was not like ours. In the Old Testament, God outlined in His laws provisions for widows and orphaned children to be taken in and cared for by other family members. In his letters, however, Paul is writing to people who have grown up in the Roman world.

In Rome, the primary purpose of adoption was to designate a strong heir rather than to provide a loving home for a child in need. If you wanted to adopt a slave, you would first have to free that slave, making them a citizen. This progression beautifully parallels our entrance into God's family. We were born into slavery, then set free, made citizens of God's Kingdom, and finally adopted as co-heirs with Christ, our sacred brother.

In an article written for Aleteia, Ellen Mady points out some other features of Roman adoption. First, although a biological child could be disowned or rejected, an adopted child could not. The choice of adoption was permanent. In that way, the adopted child had more legal protection than even a biological child.[1]

Second, an adopted child "received a new identity. Any prior commitments, responsibilities, and debts were erased. New rights and responsibilities were taken on. Also, in ancient Rome, the concept of inheritance was part of life, not something that began at death. Being

---

1. Ellen Mady, How the Roman Practice of Adoption Sheds Light on What St. Paul was Talking About, (Aleteia 2017),

adopted made someone an heir to their father, joint-sharers in all his possessions and fully united to him."

You and I have been adopted. There was a process and there was a fee/payment. That process is implied in the Bible passages listed above: the Son was sent forth at the right time, and through the Son we received the Spirit of Sonship, the Spirit of adoption, the Spirit that teaches us to cry out, "Daddy, Father."

We've touched on Romans 3 earlier, but let's dig a little deeper.

Growing up in church and a Christian school, I was made to memorize Romans 3:23 more times than I can remember. "All have sinned and fall short of the glory of God." Okay, that's true, and it played into me believing sin was a continuous main character in my story. It wasn't until years later that I realized that I had read the following verses many times, but never connected them to verse 23. How tragic for my young mind. Read the rest of the verses and see how I was constantly reminded of the problem but was not required to ruminate with equal fervor upon the hope.

Roman 3:23-25 says, "... all have sinned and fall short of the glory of God, and are justified by his grace as a gift, through the redemption that is in Christ Jesus, whom God put forward as a propitiation by his blood, to be received by faith. This was to show God's righteousness, because in his divine forbearance he had passed over former sins."

We have discussed the blood already, so let's focus on two other key concepts contained in this passage: redemption and justification.

First, the blood. The blood of Jesus, our perfect sacrifice, was required before the foundations of the world. In Revelation 13 we are told that the Book of Life, wherein our names are written, was written before the foundation of the world and was called, "The Book of Life of the Lamb who was Slain." Quite a title—and it clearly illustrates that the price was set from the beginning. There would need to be a lamb, and that lamb would need to be slaughtered.

There is a stumbling block for us at this point, of course. The price makes no sense to our modern Western minds. I'm not saying we can't weave a beautiful theological explanation for it, I simply mean that it doesn't make sense. God was not bound by some cosmic requirement to choose that price. He was not forced by anyone or anything. Yet, this is the price he ordained, the blood of his perfect and beloved Son.

We stumble at this point because it is difficult for us to feel the value of the price. We are used to purchasing property with money. That is how we understand value. The violent death and blood of Jesus have a unique value, but outside of the church walls where we sing about it and preach about it, the shedding of someone's blood is not regarded as valuable in any transactional way.

However, the way we value the blood of Jesus is completely beside the point. Our judgment of its value does NOT matter. It was the Father's prerogative to establish the price. He set the price, the Son paid the price, and the father accepted the payment as sufficient. It is the Father's valuation that matters, not ours.

When talking about this issue I have often referenced the adoption of my youngest son. When I set out to adopt him, the price was set by the adoption agency and the government of the country I was adopting him from. I accepted that price. I paid the price. The payment was none of my son's business. He was the recipient of the goodness purchased by my payment of that price, so in that way, it was deeply his business, but neither the price itself nor the payment was his business to judge.

I cannot imagine my son coming to me, looking me in the eyes, and telling me that I don't love him and that he is not my son because "You didn't pay enough when you adopted me." That accusation would not make any sense, and I don't expect that he will ever make it. As far as I know, the cost of his adoption has never even crossed his mind. He simply knows we saw him, we chose him, and we did everything necessary to make him our son.

Whenever I struggle to accept all of the amazing things God has said about the love He has given to me, the love that calls me his child, I devalue the price of my adoption. I am questioning the value of the blood of Christ. In those moments it is not for me to understand why God prized the blood of Christ so highly: it is only for me to accept that he does value it that highly. I have to stop trying to feel the value and instead surrender to the value placed on it by the maker of the universe...my Dad.

Romans 3 tells me that through my father's gracious payment of that price, I was justified and redeemed. Redemption carries yet another implication, for to redeem something is to buy it back. The concept of redemption leads us to the cross, where Jesus, as he breathed his last before surrendering His soul said, "It is finished."

I confess that the phrase, "It is finished," is one of my least favorite English translations of that verse. What Jesus said from the cross was, "tetelestai," a word that carries a transactional meaning. It is more literally translated, "paid in full." At the moment Jesus completed paying for my adoption he cried out to the Father that the set price was paid—and not just paid, but paid in full. The deal was done. Transaction completed. The adoption was consummated. He did not simply say "It is finished," as in "I'm done dying." No! His simple declaration was a proclamation of hope and finality. You and I have been redeemed because the price has been paid in full.

As we consider God's perfect fatherly love toward us, we must remember that his love was not unconditional, something was physically done to purchase it. My belief in God's fatherly love is not just a nice notion that makes me feel better when I'm blue. My belief is an act of worship, an expression of gratitude for the most expensive adoption that ever took place in the history of the world.

Just like what happened to the status of adoptees during the days of the Roman empire, my past has been erased and I have been declared a new creature. As the Bible says, the old has passed away and everything has become new. I have been crucified with Christ. In Christ, I am a new creature. I no longer live but Christ lives in me.

This is where our adoption gets deeper and more mysterious. I am not simply adopted as I am, but because I have been crucified with Christ, killed, and resurrected, I am now clothed in the very righteousness of Jesus. The gift of God's grace has made me justified.

It is easy to confuse forgiveness and justification. When someone wrongs me and apologizes, my usual response is, "It's okay." That is a statement of justification. When you think about it, that's a strange statement. Is it really okay? Can I make it okay? If a wrong was done, it was objectively wrong, and wrong is not okay. It is not within my power to declare something wrong to be okay, so why do I say "It's okay?" Answer: because it's easier and less embarrassing for me to say "It's okay" than to say, "I forgive you."

I would rather claim the power to make a wrong right than to use the word, "forgive." Hey, maybe it's just me, but I feel pretentious and condescending saying "I forgive you." However, forgiveness is the only thing that is within my power to offer. Because of the forgiveness I have received, I cannot hold judgment over someone who has wronged me, so I forgive them. That's the only thing I can do.

But in my adoption through Christ's sacrifice, I was forgiven AND justified. Because of the person and work of Christ, my Dad looks at me and says, "You're okay." Not, "It's okay." The behavior is not okay, but I AM. I have been forgiven and more. I have been justified. I have been made right.

I can hear the protestations of some readers. "Hold on Aaron, you tricky double-talking dude. You just said that wrong is objectively wrong, that it can't be made right just by saying it is okay." Yes! That's exactly what I said! The sinfulness of sin is an objective and unchangeable fact. My Dad did not ignore that reality, but in Christ, He introduced another element to the equation, the blood of my Sacred Brother. Now the whole equation has been changed. Sin is still sin, but the expression of the Father's love is so great, that He, and only He, has the right to not only forgive but to say, "The price has been paid in full. The objective reality of sin has been paid for, not ignored. You are forgiven and YOU are okay. YOU are holy because YOU have become a new creature enlivened with the very spiritual DNA of my precious Son. You are justified."

"We have now been justified by his blood, how much more shall we be saved from God's wrath through him!" (Rom. 5:9)

"What then shall we say to these things? If God is for us, who can be against us? He who did not spare his own Son but gave him up for us all, how will he not also with him graciously give us all things? Who shall bring any charge against God's elect? It is God who justifies. Who is to condemn? Christ Jesus is one who died — more than that, who was raised — who is at the right hand of God, who indeed is interceding for us. Who shall separate us from the love of Christ? Shall tribulation, or distress, or persecution, or famine, or nakedness, or danger, or sword? As it is written, 'For your sake we are being killed all the day long; we are regarded as sheep to be slaughtered.' No, in all these things we are more than conquerors through him who loved us. For I am sure that neither death nor life, nor angels nor rulers, nor things present nor things to come, nor powers, nor height nor depth, nor anything else in all creation, will be able to separate us from the love of God in Christ Jesus our Lord." (Romans 8:31-39)

Chapter Sixteen

Order of Operation

Over the years some friends, most of them pastors, have expressed concern about my passionate emphasis on Abba theology. Their fears tend to revolve around a perceived diminution of God's holiness. They see danger if we make Him too approachable. After all, there are stories in the Bible about the sheer power of the holiness of God driving people to their faces, trembling and knowing that in the face of His holiness, they would surely die.

Moses wanted to approach God but was only allowed to see the shadow of His passing. Isaiah fell on his face and cursed himself when he glimpsed the holiness of God. And let's not forget Uzzah, who steadied the ark of the covenant so that it would not fall and was immediately struck dead because he had not taken seriously the holiness of God.

One of my favorite New Testament writers is John. When he wrote about the "Last Supper" he described himself as the one resting against Jesus' bosom. In Jesus' day, meals were taken in a reclining position. The disciples would have been propped on one elbow, feet away from the table, picking up food with the other hand. But John takes special note of his proximity to Jesus. Throughout his Gospel, he calls himself "the disciple that Jesus loved," conveying a deep sense of his intimate

connection and love for Jesus and Jesus' reciprocation of that sentiment. That is why the beginning of Revelation is so interesting.

In chapter one of Revelation, the same John who felt so free to
be physically close and emotionally connected to Jesus has a vision.
He hears a voice and turns to see someone "like a son of man" (Jesus'
favorite name for Himself), clothed with a long robe and with a golden
sash around his chest. He then describes the glorified son of man in
all of his holiness. This is the same Jesus he knew, now clothed in his
majesty. John says, "When I saw him, I fell at his feet as though dead.
But he laid his right hand on me saying, 'Fear not, I am the first and
the last, and the living one. I died, and behold I Am alive forevermore,
and I have the keys of death and Hades.'"

John's response is both appropriate and consistent with the reaction of others who caught a glimpse of God's holiness. But look at
Jesus' response. He touches John, laying His right hand on him, com-
forting him, and telling him not to be afraid. Think about that. This is
Jesus, the first and the last, the fullness of the eternal Father enfleshed.
This remarkable scene is possible because the glorified Jesus was the
same Jesus who had walked with John and had been His friend. The
sacrifice of the incarnate Christ on the cross made it possible for a
person like John, for people like you and me, to stand in the presence
of the holiness of God and live—and not only live but be loved. John
was able to both snuggle with Jesus, be terrified of Jesus, and be raised
up by Jesus when he was afraid.

I read many books about the holiness of God in my zealous youth.
I loved them. However, the greatest lesson I learned about the holiness
of God came at a Lakota sweat lodge. It was my first such experience,
and I had come at the behest of a friend. I felt completely out of place,
standing awkwardly on a hill among strangers, dressed only in my
shorts, waiting for this mysterious ceremony to begin.

I wandered over to a man who was tending a fire. Now, I have no idea whether what happened next is standard practice for a firekeeper at a Lakota sweat lodge, but here is the conversation that transpired.

Me: (awkward and out of place) Hey...whatcha up to...

Man: (with an assessing gaze) I am tending to our rock friends.

Me: (with pastoral conversational skills) No kidding. That's great...what's a rock friend?

Man: (with a patient sigh) Creator is not OF the air. That is the domain of the birds. Creator is not of the earth, for man and the beasts walk on the earth and live. Creator is not of the water, for it is in the water that the fish live and thrive. Creator is of the fire, for none can stand in the fire and not be consumed. None can dwell in the fire and survive. But our rock friends can dwell in the fire. Today our rock friends will help us to pray. Our rock friends will bring us to the fire of Creator and we will pray.

Oh, holiness! Yes, God is in the fire, the burning flame of his "otherness." His holiness is not simply a moral separation because I am a sinner and he is not. Even if I could somehow manage to live a perfect life God would still be "other" than me, above, beyond, HOLY. His holiness is the blazing reflection of His awesomeness, beauty, power, love, and gentleness.

All of his attributes are "other" and separate from me. But Jesus, our Sacred Brother, dwelt in and bore within Himself the complete fire of God's holiness and brought it to within reach of humble creatures like us. We looked at Him and beheld the holiness of God. He lifted our faces from shame and looked deep into our eyes, raised us back to our feet, and whispered, "Don't...be...afraid."

I will never forget the words of the man tending the fire. We did pray that day. For four straight hours, in the choking steam, we prayed. In the fourth round of praying, all of the remaining rock friends were brought into the sweat lodge, glowing in the pitch black of the space. At the end of our time, the man leading the sweat swept his hand over his water bucket (I assume it was a bucket, it was too dark to see) and poured all of the water over the rocks. The water hit the rocks like an explosion. Steam erupted and I thought I was going to die. The leader of the sweat cried out, "Creator help us, we cannot," and all 18 of us packed into that small space hit the dirt, faces pressed into the earth searching for air, surrendering self-sufficiency. Creator help us indeed, for we cannot.

How appropriate that the end of four hours of prayer led us to fall on our faces in desperation. How appropriate that even the reflection of my God's fire would leave me prostrate and begging for mercy, just like so many who walked before me. Just like my big brother John, I fell on my face as though dead. But stories about my Abba and me never end in death. Never.

Let's talk about order of operation, which should come first—knowing Him as holy, or knowing Him as Abba? I submit that because Jesus told us that all who would see His kingdom must come as little children, we were created to know Him first as Abba. A proper order of operation allows us to see God as bigger and bigger as we mature. Our growing awareness of His holiness does not drive us away from Him, it draws us closer to him—if we know him as Abba first.

For a person who only sees God as holy, that holiness creates distance. That person is not experiencing God in the way that was opened by Jesus. It is indeed fearful for a sinner to fall into the hands of a righteous God, but because of Jesus, I am dead to sin and alive in Christ and I can never BE a "sinner" again. The work is complete and there is now no condemnation because I am in Christ.

I am invited to boldly approach the throne of grace, even in my time of need. When am I in need of the grace that comes from the throne?

At exactly the time that I would expect and deserve condemnation for my behaviors, thoughts, and attitudes. At exactly the time that my behavior should make me terrified of approaching His holiness, I am invited to boldly approach. Not to crawl. Our tenacious clinging to believing in the love of our Abba should never diminish our understanding of His holiness but should allow us to approach the one who has invited us to approach Him.

When Jesus taught us to pray, He gave us this order of operation, the sequence that is essential for an ongoing, appropriate relationship with the Father. He told us to begin our prayer, "Daddy, who is in heaven, Your name is Holy." See how both principles are conveyed in that sentence. We are to approach Him as Abba and recognize and declare his holiness. Loop back to John's experience. He learned to snuggle first and then he experienced that which drove him to his face. If he had not known the intimate Jesus, I wonder if he could have risen when Jesus laid His hand on him and told him not to be afraid.

The intimacy I am offered with the Father does not diminish His holiness. It exemplifies it. How arrogant I have been, supposing that my groveling proved His greatness, that my shame showed the world His holiness. All the while He has been beckoning me to come, to let Jesus be enough, to let Jesus' sacrifice drive me into the arms of Him who calls me beloved, who exults over me with singing, who has carved my name on his hands. Yes, there are two tattoos that God bears. On the thigh of the son is written, "King of Kings and Lord of Lords," but on the hands of the Father...me.

In the movie remake of the musical The King and I called "Anna and the King," there was a scene where the King of Siam sat on his throne while everyone in attendance lay prostrate on the floor under the threat of death to anyone who would rise before his majesty. Yet, in the midst of the scene, his favorite little daughter scampered through the bodies, stepping over those who were paralyzed with fear and reverence. She unceremoniously climbed up onto his lap, whispered something in his ear, and scuttled away again. And the king allowed it! More, the king smiled!

The daughter had no concept that she was breaking protocol. She was not aware that the king was the lord of his hosts, commanding armies of Siam. She only knew he was her daddy, and that her daddy would not send her away.

Over time, as they grew, the king's children would discover more and more about his power and majesty. They would find themselves in awe of him. However, because they had first come to know him as their father and themselves as his beloved children, their growing awareness of his power would never cause them to doubt their special place in his affections. Their growing reverence would be in honor of him and they would feel pride, not fear that created distance.

This is what I mean by order of operation. If I do not allow myself to have a proper Abba theology, the belief that I am invited into throughout the New Testament, then God's majesty will only keep me on my face in the throne room. I will never feel the gentle hand on my shoulder and the quiet voice saying "Don't be afraid, you are my beloved. Now come and see all that I have to show you."

The beauty of this order is that it invites me to join my Father on a journey to understand and experience His holiness. I don't have to watch it alone and from a distance, like some stargazer with a telescope experiencing the vastness of the Stars through a little peephole. Discovering all that God is, in step with him, in intimacy, allows the development of my theology to be both personal and joyful, not simply fearful. Yes, it is true that "the fear of the Lord is the beginning of wisdom," but what child starts out as wise? We start out as dependent and simple. We start out gazing up into the face of a mother or father who is holding us close, rocking us gently, and calming our fears. Oh, God is fearful, but the rest of the story is that perfect love casts out fear and God so loved us that He sent His only Son to carry us to His waiting arms.

Chapter Seventeen

The Anthropomorphic Problem

At this point we need to address a common complication in our comprehension of God as father: our tendency to ascribe human characteristics to something nonhuman. The Bible is full of anthropomorphic images of God. Those are human descriptions of something not human. How could it be otherwise? Our human experience is limited to things of this world, obviously. God must describe Himself to us using familiar imagery, ideas, and words that we can wrap our minds around.

So, for example, when the Bible says that God protects us with his feathers and his wings, we don't conclude that God is some kind of bird. We know that when Jesus himself looked over Jerusalem and said, "How often have I desired to gather your children together as a hen gathers her brood under her wings," he is speaking poetically and metaphorically. But those pictures give us a sense of His character and the emotion that goes with it.

God is the ultimate illustrator. Jesus' favorite method of teaching was storytelling. God ordained feasts and holidays to paint pictures. He gave His people customs and laws to provide further explanation. At His direction, millions of animals were slain to atone for guilt, all to illustrate the cost of sin and the need for payment. All pictures, illustrations, portraits.

God used history itself to illustrate. Consider how many situations David or Isaiah found themselves in that were actually meant to foreshadow a coming event. The redemptive narrative of Israel and Israel's Messiah is a mural showing, to those who have eyes to see, the character and attributes of our Heavenly Father. Those illustrations are our tutors. If our goal is to know God, then we must enter into the great gallery of the Word. We must browse the masterpieces that have been placed there with precision and care. But we are more than spectators or visitors in the museum of God's character. We, like Mary Poppins, are invited to climb into the portraits, experience the reality they portray, and see the world as it truly is. We take the bread and drink the wine and physically consume it. We participate in Jesus' death and resurrection through baptism, a physical experience. We were created to participate, not pontificate.

One of the most deeply personal illustrations of God's heart and character is found in marriage. Both Jesus and the Father are described in the role of husband.

Revelation 19:7 says, "Let us rejoice and be glad and give the glory to Him, for the marriage of the Lamb has come and His bride has made herself ready." God paints a masterpiece of care and redemption in a painting called, "My Beloved," in Ezekiel 16:1-14. God's jealousy for His people is sketched in marriage. Christ's return is portrayed as a groom making ready His home for His bride in John 14:3. When you experience marriage as God intended it, you discover your Lord in a special way. You will find Him and feel Him and honor Him in your new creation with your spouse.

Now here is a funky question: Did God make marriage and then think to himself, "Hey, that's a great way to show how I feel about them. I should use that!" Or did he create us with that relationship so that we would have the opportunity to discover who He is a little more clearly? After all, it was not necessary for Him to create us as couples.

Whenever I raise this point, the first rejoinder is usually, "Yeah, but we needed to be married so that we could procreate." But that is simply not true. We could have been created in any number of ways, as nature itself shows. There are thousands of asexual species that do not need a partner to procreate. We could have experienced life and procreation without marriage if God had chosen that method for us. Yet, we are given marriage, and then God explains that through marriage we can understand some of His longing, His jealousy, His love, and His sacrifice.

Now we come to the portrait of the Father, an anthropomorphic painting that is as important and foundational as any we could have been given. But here too we run into a problem. God is not a man.

For a number of years, I routinely asked people to close their eyes and picture God. Most of them described an older wise-looking man, definitely bearded. There is a good reason for that picture. The Bible gives God male pronouns throughout Scripture, and Daniel does indeed give his image of the Ancient of Days a wooly white beard.

Still, God is not a man. He is, as the theologians would say, "transcendent." John 4:24 says, "God is spirit, and those who worship Him must worship in spirit and truth." And in Numbers 23:19, "God is not a man, that He should lie, nor a son of man, that He should change His mind." In other words, He is not one of us. The very heart of His Holiness is His separateness. He does not carry the XY chromosomes that make a man a male.

It is because of God's infinite nature that He had to use finite terms to reveal Himself to us in the Bible. We could never comprehend God as He is, so He showed us in terms we could comprehend. The condescension of Jesus dwelling in the flesh is the ultimate expression of the divine defined in humanity.

The danger of our mistake in making God a man, as I am a man, is that if I believe that God is a male and I am a male, then somewhere in the back of my mind I believe that God and I share something that my wife cannot share with Him. Somehow the image God stamped on my life as a man is a little closer to God's heart than my female counterpart. God and we boys have a club that the girls can't join.

I believed that this paradigm never affected me outright. I never felt that I was some kind of chauvinist or a "he-man woman-hater." I was not even conscious of the thought, but I do believe I subtly devalued women because I misunderstood this principle and I believe women have often devalued themselves. How could we not? According to my misconstruction of the God of the universe, I was more special than them, even if I never would have said it. I believed, subconsciously, that she had more to gain in observing my life and relationship with God than I had to learn from her.

Let's go a little deeper. In Genesis 1 we read, "Then God said, "So God created man in his own image, in the image of God he created him; male and female he created them." We first note the plurality of the word "man" as it is used there. The word "Adam" in Hebrew does not necessarily carry with it a masculine quality. It can mean man in the sense of a male person or, just as it does in the English language; it can mean man in the sense of "mankind" or "any human." It is the second meaning that is intended in that verse.

This is no trivial point. It goes to the heart of understanding what being made in God's image means. "Man" is not used in reference to Adam himself in Chapter 1, but rather to both Adam and Eve. The verse further clarifies this for us. "And God created man in His own image, in the image of God He created him; male and female He created them." The word used for "in the image of God He created him" does not carry with it a gender. It is simply a word that points to the subject of the verb. In Genesis 1:22 the same word is translated as "them" and refers to both male and female animals. So here in Genesis, we see that it was neither man nor woman who bore their creator's image alone.

In Genesis 5:1-2 God rearticulates that fact. "This is the book of the generations of Adam. In the day when God created man, He made him in the likeness of God. He created them male and female, and He blessed them and named them man in the day when they were created."

So men and women are co-bearers of the image of God, he no more than she, and she no more than he. In one another we have the opportunity to discover God's character in ways that we never could alone.

In 1 Corinthians 11, Paul is talking about men and women and he says, "For a man ought not to cover his head, since he is the image and glory of God, but woman is the glory of man." Do you see it? He says that man was made in the image and glory of God. Check, we got that. But then he talks about the woman. He does not say that she was made in the image and glory of man, because she wasn't. She was created from a part of him, but she was never created in his image, for she was made in the image of God, not Adam.

So why are we belaboring this point? The statement that God is not male is not controversial. Almost every version of theology affirms that God is spirit, not human. But it starts to become more controversial when we affirm that God, with all of His male pronouns (anthropomorphic) has as many feminine qualities as male qualities, for both man and woman were made in His image. And to go one step further, His qualities as Father include all that it means to be a mother.

When the book, "The Shack," came out, this very idea was a major bone of contention. That God the Father was portrayed as a woman. I'm not going to get into a book critique here, love the book, hate it, not my business. I will only point out that this issue of allowing God to have mother qualities seems to be uncomfortable for many people.

Try to not get stuck in the weeds on this. It's a simple concept. God has put His image in men and women as co-image bearers. God has given us mother and father pictures and experiences and feelings that help us understand Him more completely.

Many people carry wounds from their mothers. For them, discovering the love of their Father without minimizing the important image of God in motherhood is vitally important. God carrying the fullness of motherhood is not a demeaning thing. Beyond that, we would miss out on some of the greatest parts of God's Fathering if we were to relegate him to the stereotype of a macho and manly dad. He is so much more than that.

God has many names in Scripture that help to give us a sense of His character. One of those names is El Shaddai. It is typically translated as "almighty God" in our Bibles. It is not entirely clear what the translation should be, it was not a common Hebrew word, but the root of the name is "shad," which means "breast." The proper translation, according to some scholars, is actually "the many-breasted one." I know that seems weird at first blush. If you search the Bible for all the places where the name El Shaddai is used, "almighty God" is appropriate, but what does it mean to have all might? It certainly carries with it the capacity of having what is needed for every situation, being sufficient. That idea is closely related to a breastfeeding mother, who has within her everything necessary to sustain her child. Whatever the child takes is replenished for the next feeding. And beyond the practical nourishment, breastfeeding is intimate. It requires touch and close contact.

The first person I heard discuss God in this way was a man who had spent years studying the names of God. The image was rather jarring to me, since El Shaddai, Almighty God, had always seemed like such a big, burly, masculine image. It took a while for me to see God in such an intimate, nurturing, light.

I don't know what God intended in that name, and since Scripture doesn't make it clear, I don't think it's our job to pretend we know. However, I love that I have a heavenly Father who draws me to His bosom, a Father who supplies all of the nurture that only a mother can give. I love that my Dad is not lacking in half of the parenting gifts. He is complete in all of the ways I have experienced imperfectly in my relationships with my mom and dad.

We will be sticking with the word Father throughout our journey, but don't be afraid to let Abba soothe your heart in ways that only a mother can.

Chapter Eighteen

The Perfect Father

So what does a perfect father look like? Let us take this out of the spiritual and theological realm for a moment and just consider a human father. Earlier I reminded you that you do not need to have experienced a perfect father to know what one looks like. So, with that in mind, take a little time to answer the questions below with your best ideas about a perfect father. (If you need to think in terms of a perfect mother for one reason or another, then go for it. This is your journey.)

Two notes: First, don't skip this step. What comes next will make sense and be personal to you if you take your time here. Second, don't over-spiritualize this. We are looking for simple answers about an earthly parent. No one is grading this.

What is he like in general:

(Sitting home at night, how does he act? Does he laugh a lot? What does his laugh sound like? Does he sit on the couch buried in the newspaper? Does he sit in his special chair and watch his children play, or does he spend most of his time on the carpet playing with them? Is he physically affectionate with his kids? Etc.)

Is he easily impressed?

(When his child paints a stick figure or an ugly house, does he frame and hang it? Does he post it on the refrigerator? When his child stammers through a speech at school, what does he feel?)

What does he do and how does he react when his kid succeeds:

(Picture his child getting the "A" on the test he was studying for, hitting his first single on the baseball diamond, standing up for a kid who was being picked on, Etc.)

What does he do and how does he react when his kid fails:

(Not when his kid sins, but when he fails, meaning things didn't work out as planned. She gets a shot at the final goal in a soccer game and misses. He studies hard and gets a "D-" on her test. Etc.)

What is his dearest hope for his child?

What does he do and how does he react when his kid sins:

(when his child willfully does wrong, how does he react? Bear in mind, as you write, that there may be an important difference between discipline and punishment. Why does he even care that his child sins?)

What is the thing that would cause him to stop loving and hoping for his child?

What causes him to be disappointed in his child?

What does he do when he is disappointed for his child?

Well done. Hopefully, you made it through all the questions and that some of them challenged you. Now I want to take you back through those same questions, sharing some of the answers I have received from others in the past so that you can hear some of the common themes.

What is he like in general?

I see him at home "present" with all of us in the family. That means that he would be with us in all we do and would be on the floor playing with us, or at the table eating with us, or in the bedroom when we are scared at night.

He would be physically affectionate. He loves to give and get big hugs. He puts a hand on me. He is not afraid of physical touch

He would respect my feelings and not be afraid or withdraw from me in those times when I need to cry out.

He laughs a lot, with a loud, contagious belly laugh.

Another wrote,

Always engaged with his kids.

Even when he's not around them he's bragging about them and sharing pictures.

When he's home there's nothing he wants more than play with them and listen to them.

He's never too busy.

He's physically affectionate.

He laughs a lot, a sincere giggle that turns to a belly laugh.

He's strong and feels safe and protective, but he's not a giant I'm afraid of.

And still another wrote,

Engaged and interested in whatever the child is up to.

Great sense of humor. On the carpet playing.

Physically affectionate.

Overall, the common threads through the hundreds of answers I have received included a sense of safety, an openness with expressed emotions, permission to laugh or cry without reservation or shame, and generosity with appropriate physical touch. The perfect father is never described as bored with the child. He is willing to play at the developmental level of his children and talk about things they are interested in. He is present in the family's life. Note, no one who answered these questions ever said that the perfect father expected his children to talk about his work or issues all or even most of the time.

Is he easily impressed?

He is easily impressed.

He genuinely celebrates even small things.

He judges his children based on their abilities, not his.

Another wrote,

Leaps up and down, physically showing his delight.

It doesn't take much to impress him.

You have to love the candor on this one

He is easily impressed by his kid.

Kid's capability has nothing to do with it.

He frames shitty artwork.

He loves talking about his kid.

You can see what was important to this respondent

He is easily impressed and vocal about his pride. When he feels it, he says it.

I have never talked through this worksheet with an individual who did not say that a perfect father is easily impressed. Everyone knows that great parents see their child's successes, small though they may be, as significant and wonderful. I had entire hallways lined with my children's drawings when they were kids, not because they were great works of art but because they came from the hearts and minds of my kids. I specifically remember one picture that my oldest drew. Its significance was that he had drawn a nose on the face for the very first time. I remember celebrating his genius and making a big deal of that developmental milestone. No one else would have seen and felt what that picture made me feel as a dad to a little dude. That picture made it up on the wall. This point may seem obvious and insignificant, but hold on because it's coming back around and it is vitally important.

When his kid succeeds

He feels pride, but his pride is for the child. He doesn't make it about himself.

He celebrates with them. "Let's get ice cream!"

Another wrote,

Praises them.

Rewards them.

Hugs them.

Feels pride and joy.

Pride is "them" focused and also feeling good that it is "his kid" who did it.

Are we seeing a thread yet?

Proud - excited and filled with joy.

Jumping up and down, expressive.

Communicates pride verbally and with details.

Gives hugs.

One more...

Relishes in the victories.

He feels respect, admiration, and pride. "That's my kid!"

Every answer I have ever received in this category includes some sense of joy and pride. The perfect father is not apathetic when it comes to the success of his child. Again, these successes do not have to be big or even something that others would applaud. The perfect father just loves seeing his child experience the joy of tasting the fruit of their labor. I also find it beautiful when people write about the physicality of the father's Joy. The jumping up and down, the hugs, the verbal praises. This father is uninhibited. The child never has to guess what he is feeling.

Notice the direction of the father's pride in these answers. I enjoyed coaching my youngest son's soccer team for many years. As he got older, I encountered more and more fathers whose pride in their child's skill was directed at themselves. It is all too common for parents to try to vicariously live their lives through their children and to try to co-opt their child's success to augment some lack in their own identity. The perfect father is perfectly secure in himself and has no need to steal the glory of his child's success.

When his kid fails

He still expresses his pride and love.

He comforts them and lets them know it's OK.

The child always knows that the father won't give up on them or abandon them.

He relates to their pain and failure. He knows how it feels, and relates to the pain.

He helps them with a plan and training to succeed in the future.

The perfect father knows when to hold the child, when to encourage, and when to just sit there and shut up and let the kid cry.

Another wrote,

First, he would validate my sadness or hurt in the failure.

He would help me talk through it and challenge me to understand why I'm feeling the way I am. He wouldn't fix it for me but would help guide me toward clearer insights. Then he would challenge me to think of ways I can adjust my behaviors rather than moving to resentment.

He would hold me in his arms in my sadness.

He would not try to fix me but would rather walk in it with me.

A perfect father is able to just sit there in silence and not feel uncomfortable.

Another wrote,

Doesn't shame the kid because of his expectations.

Gives perspective to the failure.

Knows when to make plans and use words for future success.

There are several things that a perfect father might do when his child fails to achieve a goal. It is right that he would give comfort. It is right that he would try to inspire them to try again. It is right that he would help them make a plan for how to succeed the next time. The theme that runs through these answers is that a perfect father knows which act of love should be implemented at each specific time. We have all been in a situation where someone's attempt to give us a pep talk to leverage us out of our grief has just felt cruel. I find the common answers to this question about the perfect father very interesting because they highlight his great sensitivity to what that particular child needs, and when it is the appropriate time to give it.

What is his dearest hope for his child?

Before I share the answers that others have given to this question, let us unpack it a little bit. Usually, when I ask it, people's initial responses are statements like, "He wants them to be happy," "He wants them to be good," and "He wants them to know God in their lives." Those are all good answers, but there is one answer that includes those and far more.

A perfect father knows his child, their gifts, and their identity better than the children can see for themselves. The perfect father wants his children to experience the fullness of life as they were created to live it. In other words, a perfect father would not want an artistic child who is bad at math to become an accountant so that she would have financial security. Further, a perfect father would not want his child's life to be free of pain, when pain helps to forge the character and uniqueness that God has placed within them. Although it hurts him to watch them walk through various stages of their life, what he most deeply desires for his children is that they become more and more the people God created them to be. That, of course, includes their relationship with their creator, the things that will bring them true joy, and the joy of being responsible for the things and relationships that have been entrusted to them.

With that in mind, here are some of the answers my friends and I have worked through as we muddled through this question.

The father's dearest hope is that his children would discover the joy of becoming more and more completely themselves, enjoying their gifts, delighting in serving others and God, with them, and experiencing life completely.

That they know that they are loved and matter/special/unique/valuable intrinsically.

And,

That they would be attuned to their heart and experience a deeper and deeper becoming of who they are and have been created to be.

That they would know how valuable they are to God and that they matter.

They would know that they are loved and cherished for who they are and not for what they can do for the father.

They would know that he is with them at every moment in life and that he would do anything to protect them.

And,

His dearest hope is that they would live life fully, through all of its ups and downs, using their gifts and discovering their passions.

Some of the pushback I have received on this line of thinking has involved the perceived danger that children who are encouraged to become fully themselves will focus solely and selfishly on their own needs and journey. Practically speaking, however, the reality is the exact opposite. We are all created with unique gifts and passions with which we serve others. A child could not become most fully themself if they were to bury those gifts and only serve themselves. On the flip side, a child could spend a lifetime serving in the church and engaging in whatever ministry people put in front of her, and still never use the gifts that God gave them to serve the body of Christ. In such a life, where sacrifice, service, and perceived selflessness were always present, the person would never discover the joy of her unique creation. That would break a father's heart.

Again, for a child to become all they were created to be requires sacrifice, love, and connection to their Heavenly Father. He or she would not experience their unique creation without those things. Selfishly pursuing their own ambition is never the definition of becoming what God intended for them. The perfect father would be brokenhearted if his child spent their life in selfless service and lost themself in the process. It is not an either-or situation. Scripture calls us to use the gifts that we have been given to be a part of the body of Christ and to be the physical hands of God, lavishing the manifold facets of God's grace on the world so that they will experience Him.

When his kid sins

This question also requires some context. I included the question "Why does a perfect father care about his child sinning?" for a reason. When I was a child, I sometimes spent time with friends whose families were very permissive and "progressive." Those parents believed that most behaviors were acceptable and part of the child's learning process. They took a hands-off approach to things that others would call sin.

So why should a perfect father care about his child sinning? In my own life, I have encountered authority figures who cared about my behavior because of how it would reflect on their institution—their school, church, or family. "Don't do that," they would say. "You'll embarrass us, you'll make us look bad." The perfect father is not insecure and would not care about his child's sin for such a shallow reason.

A parent might also be concerned that his child's sin would hurt other people. Collateral damage is certainly a real consequence of sin, but if that is the primary reason that a father cares about his child sinning then it shows he cares more about everyone else than he cares about his child. The perfect father would certainly grieve damage done to others, but that emotion would never be detached from his concern about what is going on with his child.

In the Gospel, the penalty for sin has been paid for, so the concern about sin is separate from a fear of judgment. So where does that leave us?

It brings us back to our answers about what the perfect father desires most for his child. Isaiah tells us that sin separates us from our God. As Christians, we realize that is not an eternal separation but a relational one. Sin takes up space in our lives and keeps us from experiencing the fullness of what God has for us and who He has made us to be. Sin causes damage to the relationships we are in and keeps us from experiencing and enjoying those beautiful gifts. Yet grace and growth triumph even in our sinful behaviors, and the perfect father sees that as well. With that in mind, here are some of the answers that our friends gave:

The perfect father cares about his child's sinful behavior because it is taking them out of the abundant journey of discovering and experiencing life as they were uniquely created to experience it.

He allows for consequences to teach the child.

He always disciplines in order to teach the child. Punishment is only employed when it aids in teaching and growing.

The sin does not affect his love for the child or change any part of their identity, and he will always convey his affection, even while dealing with sin, communicating in a way the child understands and believes.

Another wrote from the perspective of a perfect mother,

The parent is able to communicate and talk through what happened and what was felt.

Not condemning or shaming.

Honest about their own experiences.

A perfect mom is always about discipline and not just punishment.

She knows the best tool to use to help teach the child.

The perfect parent cares about sin because it is keeping their child from the fullness of life.

Someone else wrote,

He would connect with the child and figure out what's going on beneath the surface.

He would help figure out a path for the future.

His goal is to teach. Different means are used to achieve that goal, such as consequences, grace, and punishment.

Finally,

He knows the child and what is appropriate and helpful in dealing with them.

He wants to see repentance, a change of mind.

He finds a balance between natural consequences and punishment, always for the purpose of teaching the child.

He cares about sin because he knows it leads to pain and suffering for the child and others.

One of the important threads through these responses is the difference between discipline and punishment. Ultimately the distinction came down to this: discipline always has the purpose of teaching, while punishment is retaliatory (ie. you did this sin, which simply necessitates this consequence to balance the scales). Everyone I questioned agreed that the perfect parent is always most concerned with teaching rather than simply punishing. There were, however, various opinions about how the perfect parent would employ punishment, allowing consequences, but including grace and mercy as a teaching tool as well. This brings us back to the deep truth that the perfect father knows his children and knows what tool would serve best to help them find abundant life once again when they have lost their way.

What is the thing that would cause the perfect father to stop loving and hoping for his child?

This is a palette-cleansing question, especially after the hard work of addressing the sin question. The general answers came down to these.

NOTHING.

Even in my rejection or rebellion, he would never stop loving or hoping for me to be the best version that I have been called and created to be.

What causes him to be disappointed in his child?

I personally struggled with the answer to this question for years. I wanted to believe that being disappointed was some kind of weakness. That if a dad was strong enough, he would be above that. That messed with my theology.

I would read passages where Jesus seemed frustrated, making statements like, "O faithless and twisted generation, how long am I to be with you? How long am I to bear with you?" I spent years trying to preach around those verses and avoid admitting any disappointment Jesus might have felt while walking this earth. Then, while preaching through Mark a number of years ago, I reached the end of my rope and stopped to really consider if disappointment is actually a bad thing.

My first epiphany came when I considered whether there were any people who could not disappoint me. Absolutely! The random stranger in line at the supermarket can't disappoint me. They can annoy me, but they cannot disappoint me because I don't know them and don't care about them. People I don't care about cannot truly disappoint me. Only people I love and have hope for can disappoint me. The potential for disappointment is part of loving someone and being in a relationship with them. Thus, if a perfect father can't be disappointed, it would only mean that he doesn't care.

That said, there is a world of difference between being disappointed IN someone and being disappointed FOR someone. So in a way, this is a bit of a trick question. To be disappointed in someone is to think less of them, to diminish their identity in your own mind. To be disappointed FOR someone is to have had a hope for them that is going unrealized, to have desires for them that they are willfully crushing in some way. With that in mind, here are some of the answers that our friends came up with:

Nothing would cause him to be disappointed IN them, because he will never think less of them, but he can be disappointed FOR them.

Anything that keeps his children from becoming fully themselves breaks his heart and he is hurt and disappointed, but he never loses hope and keeps pushing for the best, patiently waiting for it and still seeing his child as everything that is most true about them.

His response doesn't push the child away. He pursues them and draws them in.

Another wrote,

When they live any version of life that is less than what they were created for, the perfect father is disappointed.

Similarly,

When they are making choices that are making them miss out on the life they were created to live.

With an interesting clarification,

If they aren't realizing their full potential, gifting, and talents. His feeling is focused on the child.

With a few more specifics,

He is never disappointed IN them because, even in their failure, their identity is still secure

He is disappointed FOR them any time they make choices to live in a manner that is less than and unworthy of all of the beautiful things he knows about who they really are.

When I act out in isolation in order to protect myself and my feelings and do not reach out for help.

Continuing to try and do it by myself rather than leaning on him or others to be with me and know me as he does.

What does he do when he is disappointed for his child?

He experiences sadness and pain.

Tries to help them see the fullness of life and how they were created.

Waits patiently for them to figure it out.

Another wrote,

He sits with me and points out my actions that caused disappointment, calls bullshit bullshit, and asks me where I am in that moment and where I hope those actions will lead me.

He would intently listen to me, allowing me to express myself and provide a safe place with the freedom to be honest and fully known.

He would challenge me to see the difference between where the path I am on is taking me, and the path that leads toward abundant life.

His facial and non-verbal expressions would invite me to be intimate and vulnerable. No judgment, always love, and compassion.

A third said,

He moves towards his children and pursues them.

Communicates their identity. "This is who you are, and what you are doing is robbing you of the joy and glory of living that reality."

He reaffirms his absolute love, that even in disappointment none of his affection and desires have diminished.

He grieves with them.

He is patient even when the child does not see the destruction of life that their behavior is causing, and remains a consistent voice of love and true identity throughout.

He knows that he can see more than the child, so he is understanding about their lack of maturity and their short-sightedness.

The common thread through these answers is that the perfect father presses in instead of pushing away. Rather than shaming, he offers an invitation to a better life, and he always has his child's identity firmly in mind. His love is secure.

So that is our description of the perfect father. How do you feel about your answers? Are you finding areas that you want to amend in your answers? I would recommend that you write out or type out a new list that you can print and carry with you. Read on, and you'll find out why. Don't pass up the opportunity to go back through your answers as you re-read some of the answers from those who went before you on this path. The clearer and more concise that you make this list for yourself, the easier the next steps will be. Besides, this is a short book and no one cares how fast you get through it. Take your time.

Chapter Nineteen

How Much More So

Now that we have finished our perfect father worksheets, I have a confession to make. This perfect father experiment was not my idea. In Matthew and Luke Jesus draws the comparison between what we know of good earthly fathers and who our Father in Heaven is. He asks the simple questions, "If your son asked you for bread would you give him a stone? If he asked for an egg would you give him a scorpion? If he asked for a fish would you give him a snake?" He then said, "If you then, who are evil, know how to give good gifts to your children, how much more will your father who is in heaven give good things to those who ask him."

How much more? The best we can imagine about the behavior and love of a perfect father only scratches the surface because our Father in Heaven is much more! What an incredible statement.

Here is the first thing I want you to do with your perfect father sheet. You can use the answers I shared from my conversations with others if you like, but if you rewrote your own on a separate sheet of paper, even better. Look at that list of characteristics of a perfect father and highlight or circle all of the ones that you have not believed about God's behavior or thoughts towards you, or that you find difficult to accept. Be as honest as you can, and remember that you are not saying that you don't believe them to be true, just that they feel unnatural or difficult to believe. Do that now.

No, seriously, don't keep reading. Go do that first. I told you, we aren't rushing here, we are working!

OK, I'm trusting you on this one. Consider, without shame, what it means that aspects of my perfect father worksheet do not match up with my understanding of God. Many of us feel like much of what is written on that sheet is very pedestrian and beneath God. For example, young children can talk endlessly about some cartoon they watched or picture book that they read. It seems normal to believe a parent would patiently listen and even enjoy it, but then when I consider whether God wants me to tell him (also known as prayer) about a movie I really liked, that seems dumb. God doesn't want to hear me talk to him about how cool I thought a movie was. He is only into Spiritual stuff.

Do you see it? I believe that a good parent wants to listen and engage in small things as well as big, but I don't believe God wants to. If I believe God doesn't want to do what a good parent would want to do, then that means I believe He is a bad father. My perfect father worksheet shows me very specifically where I have come to believe that God is not at all like a good father. Sadly, for most people I've talked to, those discrepancies were in the small, beautiful, intimate areas of fatherhood. In other words, God just can't be bothered unless it's big, Spiritual, and important.

Those characteristics that you marked on your worksheet, the ones that are hard to believe that God feels about you or behaves toward you are the accuser's playground, his dance club, and party central. They are the areas in your life that you will most easily accept condemnation. Your highlights show you the places where you struggle to let God love you well.

As I have watched individuals do this task, I have noticed that most people have trouble believing that God is actually interested in them personally. If they grew up in the church, they have often seen God as primarily focused on His kingdom. Their primary function, therefore, was to work in furthering His kingdom. In that way of thinking, God becomes a workaholic who only has kids in order to staff the family business. That father doesn't particularly like when we take time off for a vacation or when we have needs that don't directly move his plans ahead. This version of parenting did not appear in anyone's description of the perfect father, that would be a terrible father. And yet it is so easy for many of us to believe that it is what our Father in Heaven feels about us and what He exclusively wants to talk about with us.

Is God concerned about his kingdom? I don't think scripture affirms that God is concerned so much as He is passionate about it, and that is an important distinction. It comes down to God's sovereignty. Understanding God's sovereignty helps us step into our rightful place as his children. Allow me to offer an illustration.

I enjoy cooking. Even when they were very young, I loved having my children with me in the kitchen. I recall a time when my oldest son, who was only four or five years old, asked to cook with me. Now, if you have experienced cooking with a young child, you know that it is not a time-saving proposition. Allowing a child to participate in the culinary arts is an act of love and not practicality. On that particular day, I decided that omelets would be a safe bet.

I had plenty of eggs, so I got a chair for my son to stand on at the counter, gave him a bowl, and told him to start cracking away. In the meantime, I withheld the number of eggs I needed and cracked them into my bowl. I successfully cracked all of my eggs without incident. My son, however, was another story. Out of the dozen or so eggs I had given him, only a couple were useful to our final product. That was okay. Whenever he crushed an egg, shells and all, into his bowl, we could simply throw that one away. And when he successfully cracked an egg, we could put that one into my bowl. We were never in jeopardy of failing to make our omelets due to his lack of egg-cracking skills. I knew what he was capable of and I knew what I needed to ultimately make our omelets.

I had cut up and prepared the fillings for our omelets, and when the time came he was able to sprinkle them into our eggs. I stood close by, making sure that he distributed the fillings in the proper amounts. A few flips and turns and—voila!—Team Us, breakfast was served.

The bottom line of the story is this: I was sovereign over my omelet. The omelet was always going to turn out the way I planned because I knew how to make an omelet.

The hard truth is that my son was never useful to me. Sure, I used some of his work, but it would have been faster and required fewer eggs if I had not used him at all. No, my son was not useful. But he was delightful. I had a grand time in the kitchen cooking with him listening to the Beach Boys turned up loud. Sit with that truth for a minute. My cute kid was not useful to me, but man did we have a good time because he was my little dude and I think he's delightful to this very day.

When I was growing up in the church, I believed that I was somehow supposed to be useful to God and his kingdom. What a dangerously arrogant thought. Did I really believe that there was anything I was bringing to the table that he could not do better himself? And if He can do everything I can do better than me then what is my purpose? The reason I call it a hard truth is that, for some of us, realizing that we are not useful to God feels like a kind of death. What do I replace it with?

The obvious reality is that, indeed, there is nothing I can do FOR God that He could not do for Himself and infinitely better. So that cannot be the point. It CAN NOT be the point. I am not useful to God, but I am delightful, and he loves to have me in the kitchen breaking eggs. Some of my efforts will make it into the mix and others were just a good time with Daddy. Look back at your list and which attributes are difficult to believe about your Abba. I'm guessing that many of the ruts you are stuck in revolve around a belief that God is focused on your utilitarian usefulness for His Kingdom and that believing that He delights in you is hard.

Freedom comes in two ways when I finally accept that I am not useful but that I am incredibly delightful. First, there is the freedom that comes with knowing that God is sovereign over his omelet. At no point in my life am I in jeopardy of messing up God's plans. If I ever again hear a pastor say, "You might be the only Jesus that person ever meets," it will be too soon. What a ridiculous thought! God is somehow hamstrung by my effectiveness and ability to serve as Jesus to someone else? God stands watching with bated breath, waiting to see if I will succeed or fail while that person's eternal status hangs in the balance? Rubbish. Complete and utter rubbish. I can enjoy Kingdom work with my Daddy knowing that He never placed the fate of humanity or the souls of other people in my hands, but has invited me into the family business to experience and enjoy everything that Kingdom work will bring.

I can just hear old friends' responses to that kind of freedom. "If people believed that then they would never tell people about Jesus!" No? Why not? "Because there would be no urgency!" Hmm, OK. You know what reader, I'm not even going to explain how sad that line of thinking is, I think you would have more fun figuring it out if you aren't seeing it right away. Let's keep talking about freedom.

Freedom also comes when I surrender to the Father's loving heart. For me to accept that I am not useful but that I am invited into the kitchen because I am delightful, I must believe that I am delightful. I am not delightful on my merit alone, but I have been crucified with Christ and resurrected as a new creature, holy and acceptable to my Dad. Because of the person and work of Jesus, God does not condescend to love a wretched creature such as I. No, He is able to fully accept and include me because I have become righteousness of Christ in Jesus. That is a reality rooted in the eternal plan of reconciliation and the mind-blowing sacrifice of Jesus that was acceptable to the Father and accomplished my adoption as a son. I am delightful without reservation. I am delightful without any qualification except Jesus.

If I am not COMPLETELY delightful and acceptable, then JESUS' BLOOD WAS INSUFFICIENT, impotent to make me so. Do you want to say that out loud? Me neither.

Many people in church struggle to accept the softer side of our heavenly Father, his patience, gentleness, and love. Somehow many of us came to feel that God is perpetually frustrated with us. And what emotion goes with frustration? Anger. I am supposed to "be holy as He is holy," right? How often do I assume that it is simply my behavior that will make me holy or unholy, leaving Jesus out of it altogether? I forget that my holiness is based, not on myself, but on Christ. My purpose in practicing obedience is to experience more and more of my new creation in Christ, to discover abundant life, and to make space for the Holy Spirit to grow his fruit in me. Obedience and right behavior have a great purpose, but it is not to MAKE me holy. That work was already accomplished on the cross.

Let's be careful as we process this issue. We must remember that anger is not a sinful or wrong emotion. Scripture is clear that anger is an emotion that is part of God's character. The difficulty is in how we, as humans, experience anger and then project that experience onto God. So let's unpack the idea of anger for a moment so that we do not have to remove an emotion from God that the Bible affirms, but we can let it remain without making our perfect Father a perpetually seething rageaholic.

Ephesians 4 tells us to, " Be angry and do not sin; do not let the sun go down on your anger, and give no opportunity to the devil." Notice that we are not told not to be angry. Anger is a natural unconscious emotion that rises up in us due to events and data around us. One of the most consistent causes of God's anger throughout the Bible involves injustice and a lack of grace or love. When we experience something we perceive to be unjust, we feel angry. That is part of God's image in us, and it would be wrong for us to avoid or suppress that emotion.

If we see injustice or cruelty and do not experience anger, something is wrong. Such apathy does not show maturity, but a deficiency. If we were in a restaurant and I pointed to a family across the room and told you that I knew that the father at that table was abusing his child, your appropriate emotional reaction would be anger. So when I consider God's anger, I know that it is appropriate, that it arises on behalf of those that are in some way being hurt or taken advantage of. Further, I know that through the work of Jesus, I have been saved from His anger and judgment, so my Father's anger is an aspect of his character that makes me feel both safe and proud because he cares about the world I live in and the people therein.

His anger is also more complete than mine. Anger might be the right emotion with the father in the restaurant, but God's anger also takes into account all that He knows about the dad's life and wounds. If I start playing that out, God is capable of feeling anger but I can't even begin to know what His version must be like compared to mind with all of the other attributes that He holds in perfect balance. We are also told to be angry but not to sin. One sign of the Spirit's work in us is the presence of self-control. We know that God's response to evil is not flippant or reactionary. He is wise in his anger and does not cease to be compassionate, merciful, and loving simply because he also experiences anger.

Let's not forget God's omniscience. I am most inappropriate in my anger when I am caught off guard by the behavior of another person or people. I think it is safe to say that if someone were to tell me that tomorrow afternoon at 3:13 two of my children would have a fight, and if they were to tell me exactly how the battle would unfold, I would have an amazing reaction to that conflict regardless of the inappropriate behavior of my children. I wouldn't be surprised. I would have good words prepared. Quite frankly, I think it would be easy.

The anger of my perfect father is never reactionary and it is never against me. He can feel angry, hurt, or sad, but my identity is never in jeopardy because my identity is in Christ. His anger, therefore, never pushes me away but draws me in with the invitation to re-engage with Him and with abundant life. Re-engaging may include making amends to those I have hurt, but that is merely a part of the process of growing up into the man He created me to be.

One of the hardest questions for participants to reconcile is the question of whether a perfect father is easily impressed. It was easy for most people to answer yes to that. However, when they had to ask if God was easily impressed with them, a shadow fell across their souls. No. God is usually disappointed with me. No. God expects more of me. No. I don't live up to His standards. I have rarely met an individual who said yes to that. The initial pushback against God being easily impressed is often, "How can I impress a God who is infinitely higher than me, who can do everything I cannot do and be everything I cannot be?"

That may seem like a reasonable objection, but we would never apply that same standard to our own parenting, or to a perfect earthly parent. When my son drew that first picture of a face that included a nose, I wasn't impressed because I didn't know how to draw a nose on a face. My drawings, though not terribly impressive, were significantly better than my small child's. Being impressed with a child has everything to do with knowing the level they are at and seeing them take a small step forward in their skills or gifting. It has nothing to do with the skills themselves or the gifting of the parent.

Maybe we have a hard time allowing God to be the kind of parent who is delighted in his children and easily impressed by them because we misjudge the significance of our offerings or work. We make the mistake of either inflating their significance or considering them silly and small. I am writing right now as a 45-year-old man. It is easy for me to believe that God's expectations of me are those appropriate to a man and not a child. And while it is true that I have responsibilities as a man and cannot care for my family as if I were a child, my insight into God and my ability to create a piece of art that He finds impressive does not parallel my physical age.

Consider this. I was a pastor for almost 23 years. I stood in front of groups of people and attempted to open the Bible and somehow communicate the eternal character of God and His Kingdom. What percentage of what I preached do you suspect was accurate? What percentage was complete? The second question is easier to answer because I have never spoken of God's character and person with anything close to a complete explanation. It is not possible for me, a finite creature, to plumb the depths of God and to explain it in finite terms. The very idea is ridiculous. Even if I had reached 2% of a complete explanation of who God is and what He feels, I would have been a mystical genius. As far as accuracy... I believe we have the ability through the guidance of the Holy Spirit to be accurate to some degree. Did I unknowingly bring a whole lot of humanity to the spiritual things I talked about? Absolutely. Did I bring my past and my experiences into the mix? Without a doubt. How grateful are we that it is the Spirit that leads us into all truth and not me or any other pastor?

The reason I bring this up for a second time is that I would often stand in the pulpit and think, What am I doing? This is ridiculous. I took great comfort in 1 Corinthians 1, the part where Paul says, "Where is the wise man? Where is the Scribe? Where is the debater of this age? Has not God made foolish the wisdom of the world? For since in the wisdom of God the world through its wisdom did not come to know God, God was well pleased through the foolishness of the message preached to save those who believe." So I would think, Okay, as long as God and I both agree that He's happy about it but it is the foolishness of preaching, I'll keep doing it.

How then was I to picture God, my Daddy, looking on as I fumbled through the mysteries of the universe that He gave us in Scripture? I am being serious about this by the way. I often thought of God sitting behind me when I preached and I pictured him loving every second of it. He was sovereign in the making of his omelet. His Spirit would do the work of leading individual lives into truth. I was just His small delightful child making my best attempt.

The things I got wrong or the things that were incomplete did not diminish the joy my Daddy felt as I passionately talked about him with my brothers and sisters. He wasn't surprised that I didn't know everything. I am like a small child sitting on the couch picking up my dad's copy of War and Peace and deciding to thumb through it. My father comes in and smiles. His smile widens as I mention some phrases I read and found interesting. He has no expectation that I will finish the book, it's a long damn book, or that I would understand Tolstoy, but I'm pretty stinking cute sitting there with that big book, and the little that I glean from it impresses Him no end.

The God of the universe loved when I taught, and not because I was good at it or was even close to wise or right. He just loved that I showed up, did my best, and it was what I was made to do. "Go get 'em, kid," I would hear Him say, "I love you so stinking much! You are amazing." And if it were not for the fact that I knew that Jesus' person and work made that possible, I never could have believed that He actually meant it. But, again, for me not to believe that would be to declare that Jesus' blood was insufficient to make it so. Impotent to make me perfectly acceptable and delightful. Nope. Faced with the options of declaring Jesus' blood to be insufficient or surrendering to the fact that I am now delightful, I am forced to surrender to delightful.

It makes me sad to think how many of God's children see him as a raging workaholic who never thinks that anything they do is good enough. And it makes me sad for God too. If you have ever been misunderstood by a child who interprets your best effort at love as nothing but a curse, then you have an inkling of how painful this can be. I marvel at God's patience with us as we do the very same thing to Him.

I consider that one of my deepest acts of worship and love toward God is to attack my embedded notions that make him less than a perfect father each and every day. I know how good it feels when one of my children recognizes and acknowledges my love for them, and I strive to respond to my Daddy in that way. After all, he is supremely worthy to be seen and thanked for the perfect loving father that He is.

What is the best version of father you can come up with? How much more so your Father in heaven.

Chapter Twenty

Accepting the Hard Truth

As we look at our perfect father worksheet, it is easy to have good feelings about any parent who would be so gracious and attentive to a child. But let's be honest—being loved this well is hard to accept.

In Luke chapter 15 Jesus responded to a group of religious leaders who were upset because He was loving and eating with tax collectors and sinners. Responding to their dissatisfaction with the presence of sinners around a rabbi, He told a series of parables. The purpose of the stories was to show the heart of the Father toward those who are deemed unlovable. Interestingly, He included a story of a father and his two sons.

The parable of the Prodigal Son is one of the most well-worn and well-loved stories Jesus ever told. We will not make an exhaustive exposition of the story here, but because it is Jesus' description of His Father, we would be remiss if we failed to point out a few details. I learned these details from a man named Roger Williams, who had extensively researched the village culture in Jesus' time and how people living in that culture would have interpreted the parables, and was gracious to spend time talking with a very young version of me about all of my silly questions.

First, this is a story about two sons, not just one. The runaway child gets a lot of press, but the older brother who stayed home represents the Pharisees, Jesus' audience, and in that way, the older brother is really the main character. The story that Jesus told was offensive to his listeners on many levels because the father's behavior was well outside of the cultural norms of Israel 2,000 years ago. There is no way that the audience would have been rooting for the father because his responses to both of his sons' behavior were completely unacceptable. And truth be told, the perfect father Jesus described in this story offends our modern minds as well if we are being honest.

The story opens with the younger son asking his father for his share of his inheritance. The proper response to that request 2,000 years ago AND today would be, "I'm not dead yet kid, and I don't appreciate you wanting to pretend that I am to get my money." The younger son is showing an incredible lack of love or respect toward his father, and yet Jesus says, "He divided his property between them." (Notice that we have just been introduced to the older brother. He divided his property between...them.)

As the tale continues, the young son leaves home and journeys into a far country, where he squanders his inheritance. Bear in mind that the money he spends came from the liquidation of family property. In a rural Jewish setting, this was anathema. God had established laws to keep the tribes of Israel intact, and those regulations included keeping property within the family so that each tribe would grow and flourish within its own borders.

That was the reason that the oldest son would receive two-thirds of the inheritance, while all other sons would divide the last third. This practice would assure that the bulk of an estate would always remain with the patriarch of the family. Since the younger brother in Jesus's story was able to leave home with his inheritance in the form of cash, we can only imagine what the father had to do to come up with that money. He had to break his cultural and community norms, displace workers, and disrupt village life. All that to accommodate the inappropriate demand of an insolent child.

It's not as though the father was a fool. He was not unaware. He knew what kind of son he was dealing with, but he ultimately funded his foolish adventure to a far-off country. He allowed for the squandering of the estate over which he had been given stewardship. This is a common dilemma for parents. I have had countless conversations over the years with parents who are trying to figure out how to love a child without enabling their bad behavior. For most modern parents, the father's decision to grant his son's request would fall into the category of enabling, and that should feel uncomfortable.

Please, dear reader, know that this story is descriptive, not prescriptive. If you are dealing with a similar dilemma, this passage is not instructing you to fund your child's folly. It is, however, showing that God's love is frustratingly extravagant in ways that we don't feel comfortable with. His love does not seem to fear the mistakes His children make, even when He could prevent them by withholding the cash.

When next we find the youngest brother, he is living and eating with pigs in a foreign land. Oh, the Jewish irony and humiliation for the son. Jesus was being hardcore in offense concerning this boy. He would not have been loved by any listener. Here, living with pigs and gentiles, he came to his senses and started to devise a speech. His speech had three parts: 1) Father, I have sinned against heaven and before you. 2) I am no longer worthy to be called your son. 3) Treat me as one of your hired servants.

He then got up and went home.

Scripture tells us that while the youngest son was still a long way off, his father saw him and felt compassion, and ran and embraced him and kissed him. We will get to the father in a moment, but first let's listen to the younger brother's speech, which is not the one he had rehearsed. In the presence of his father's extraordinary love, his planned three-part speech became a two-part speech. "Father, I have sinned against heaven and before you. I am no longer worthy to be called your son." That statement screams about the beauty of losing our self-righteousness.

The third part of his speech had been a weak attempt to promise to earn his way and pay back what he had squandered. How sad it is when the wayward Christian returns to the father only to become his slave. How unrealistic and full of crap we can be. There was no way this kid, as a servant, could have earned the third of his father's estate that he had blown. And how much do I act like him when I pretend, for my own sake, that I could ever become God's slave and even begin to pay him back for the cross. In the face of his father's grace and love, he lost his self-righteousness and knew that he just wanted to be a son again.

But what about the father here? First, we are told that he sees the child a long way off, so we know that he's been watching and waiting. He then runs to the child. Did he run because of his love? It does seem evident from his hugging and kissing, the kind of physical affection we said would characterize the perfect father. However, his son is also returning to a village that would now loathe him.

Villagers depended on one another to live within the boundaries of cultural norms because every decision affected the daily lives of the other people in the village. These people were working for their daily bread, for their actual survival. This is not something we consider today, in a world where we can just go to the grocery store and get our food for the week, clueless about who grew it or delivered it. None of that matters in our disconnected world, but it mattered back then. The father ran to the child because of his love and, I believe, because he was aware of the danger his son would face when he returned to the village.

Next, we see the three gifts that the father gave to his youngest son. First, he calls for the best robe to be put on him. That would have been his robe. He clothed his son in his glory. That was an act of protection. Clothing his son in his robe made any attack on the son an assault on his own person. What a glorious picture of the way we are clothed in the righteousness of Christ. There is no condemnation for those who are in Christ.

Second, he calls for a ring to be put on his hand. By this, he was formally reinstating the son into the family and the business of the family. I will admit that I struggle with God's willingness to allow stupid people back into His business. I think of Peter, who swore to lowly servants outside Jesus' trial that he didn't even know Jesus. The way Jesus immediately reinstated him on the shores of the Sea of Galilee... Come on! Don't we need a probationary period? Wouldn't that be wise? Don't sinners need to prove they've changed? It's hard for me to criticize God's process when I look at all of the ways that I have been restored without probation, loved without payment, and trusted without judgment.

When I was a junior in high school I got a big kick out of the story of Samson ripping the gates from the Philistine city, carrying them 40 or so miles away, and dropping them on top of a hill. It's a hilarious story. You don't need much imagination to picture the poor Philistines following Samson at a safe distance waiting for him to put their city gates down so they could carry them all the way back.

However, I also noticed the reason Samson was in the Philistine city in the first place. He was there to have sex with a gentile prostitute.

That's odd for a biblical hero (understatement award to me please). Even more strange is that, after Samson left the prostitute and was ambushed by the Philistines, God filled him with His spirit, and that's when he ripped the gates from the city. I didn't like thinking about God filling Samson with his Spirit right after Samson had sneaked into the home of the very enemy he was supposed to be fighting in order to have sex with a prostitute.

I took this concern to a pastor who graciously spent a lot of time with me during my high school years. (Thank you, Dennis Cagle.) I told him about my disgust, and how inappropriate it was for God to impart His spirit to a man of such low moral character, especially at a time when the filling of the Spirit was rare and special.

He just smiled and said, "Yeah, makes me wonder what He will even do with a person like you."

Well, that shut me up. Still, over the years I struggled with allowing God to be this gracious with me or others. I was always more like the Pharisees at the beginning of Luke 15, who believed that Jesus was able to purchase my forgiveness at a discount since I wasn't nearly as bad as Samson, Peter, or the younger brother. Today, I am grateful to know that my needs are no less desperate than theirs. Some hit rock bottom early and turn to Christ, while others of us take a little longer and after a lot of church confusion and subsequent failure.

Finally, the father calls for shoes to be put on his son's feet. This is a statement that his son will never be a servant in the house. Servants did not wear shoes. Thank goodness the younger brother dropped the third part of the speech he had prepared back at the pigsty. His daddy did not want his child as a servant. He just wanted his boy home.

The father then announced that there would be a party at his house. This was no small thing, for parties were far more important in a village in the Middle East two thousand years ago than they are today. Imagine that you eat simple food, and not a lot of it, every day. Your diet never varies. You go to work early and work hard all day. That is your life, day in and day out. But when there is a party, the entire community attends. There is dancing and feasting and singing that sometimes lasts for days. Those celebrations were filled with joy because they were a rare break from the mundane, the monotonous, the tasteless. The women and children stood at the windows, eating and singing and dancing, and the men were inside eating and dancing with each other. I know, it doesn't sound like our kind of party, but that's the way they rolled.

The oldest son in a home would play a prominent role in the celebration ritual. In that patriarchal village society, people would have found it uncomfortable to be served by the father himself. The oldest son was a representative of the father's hospitality and generosity. His service could be accepted by the participants. (I hope you are catching glimpses of Jesus in this.) As the oldest brother greeted each new arrival to the party, he would give the greeting of the father. Then he would personally serve the guests of honor. He would bring them their food and refill their cup, and throughout the night would make toasts to the honored guests. His was a very important job.

So the party started. Now, let's go find the elder brother. Scripture tells us that the "older son was in the field, and as he came and drew near to the house he heard music and dancing. And he called his servants and asked what these things meant." Pause here. We have just heard that this older son had important duties at any party in his father's home. So why did he not run into the house to take his place and do his duty? The party had started and he wasn't even there!

The common answer is that he was angry because his younger brother was the honored guest. But that is not the case. Look again. He heard the party happening and did not know who the guest was, but instead of running into the house to fulfill his duty, he called for a servant to tell him why there was a party going on. He is dishonoring his father by his apathy and lack of haste. The older son was focused on his life outside the house. We never see the older brother enter the home at any point in this story. His life is in the fields. More on that in a moment.

It is then that he is told that the party is for his brother who has returned. The older brother was outraged. Scripture says, "He was angry and refused to go in." You can see this grown man keeping his distance, throwing a tantrum, standing on his principles, and refusing to participate in a party thrown by his father. Don't think of this like a modern parent; kids get away with that level of disrespect every day in our culture. The culture of Jesus' day did not permit a child to be disrespectful without concequence.

At that point, cultural norms gave the father two options in dealing with his oldest son. He could ignore the disrespect and go on with the party without him. You can just imagine the gossip in the village next week, but the father could choose to bear it. His other option would be to leave the house (which would make it necessary for everyone to leave with him, because it would be inappropriate to keep partying in the patriarch's house while he is elsewhere), go out to his inappropriate son, and beat him in front of everyone. In that case, the villagers would nod and say, "Now there is a good father."

The father in Jesus' story made his choice. Scripture says that he chose to leave. Picture the party following along. But here again, the father goes off the rails. He did not leave the house to confront the child's wickedness in a culturally appropriate way. Jesus said that he came out and entreated, and pleaded, with the older brother to come in and join the party. What! How humiliating! How scandalous for all of the onlookers to see a father pleading with a wicked child to come enjoy a party. Even in our culture, you're not supposed to reward bad behavior with parties.

And then it gets worse.

The older brother said to his father, "Look." We don't even have to move past the first word of what the older brother said to see his disrespect, his condescension, and his dismissal of his father. "LOOK here, old man. LOOK, you don't get it. LOOK...open your eyes. LOOK." That word disgusts me and breaks my heart every time I read his opening gambit.

Then he says some of the most tragic words recorded in Scripture. "All these years I have slaved for you." "All these years I have served you." Do you see it? This boy imagines that he has no place in the home, only in the fields where we find him. His view of his relationship with his father is that of a slave, of a servant, not a son. He then makes a self-righteous claim. "I never disobeyed your command, yet you never gave me a young goat that I might celebrate with my friends. But when this son of yours came, who has devoured your property with prostitutes, you killed the fattened calf for him."

All of his statements are statements of entitlement based on his work. None of them are based on the identity of a child, a son. "I've slaved for you. I've never disobeyed you. I'm owed a party. And the fact that you aren't giving me what is due is a crime against me." Further, notice how he positions himself in relation to his brother. "This son of yours," he says. He wants nothing to do with any connection to that wicked child. It's not his brother, just his father's son. Even within that statement, there is an accusation. He's yours. Somehow this is your fault.

I can hardly imagine the thoughts that went through the minds of Jesus's audience when they heard these statements by the older brother. Don't forget, the older brother is the character who represents the religious Pharisees and scribes. Also, remember that the older brother is now voicing what many in the audience must have been thinking. This is a bad dad. He's too indulgent. He's breaking all of the cultural rules. Who are we supposed to root for in this confusing story?

"And he (the father) said to him, 'Son...'" We have to stop there and notice that the word he uses for "son" is the same word he uses when talking about us. It is the affectionate teknon, the intimate word for his precious boy. Even here, the father's tenderness and affection have not diminished even slightly. Think back to our perfect father worksheet and realize that it was not an "unbiblical" perspective on the tenderness and patience of our Daddy.

"Teknon, you are always with me, and all that is mine is yours. It was fitting to celebrate and be glad, for this your brother was dead, and is alive; he was lost, and is found."

The father is both gracious and practical. Remember that at the beginning of the story he "divided his property between them." The older brother was present at the beginning of the story, and at that time he took his inheritance just like the younger brother. He was a villain from the start. He ran away from his father's home too. He only ran as far as the fields. Just like the younger brother, he tried to pay his own way, just by becoming a slave to the most gracious and gentle father ever.

The older brother's rebellious journey did not take him to foreign lands, only to the back acreage and his work. The father now reminds him that everything belongs to him, despite his ingratitude. He could have a party anytime he wants. Further, his outburst about not getting to have a party with his friends is just silly. Who were the people partying inside? His village. His friends were already inside having a party. It is so sad to see how our bitterness turns into illogical isolation.

The story ends with the father reminding the older brother who he is. He is a child who is in possession of all of the riches that the father has and he has a place inside the house where the party continues.

Although I love the behavior of the father in this story, I fear that if a parent I knew behaved like this toward either kind of child described in the parable, I would judge them as far too lenient and would probably consider them to be a bad parent. Jesus is demanding that we face a father unlike any that we would feel comfortable with. And how ironic that the great discomfort comes from his extraordinary ridiculous love that is steeped in the indescribable grace that we talked about earlier in this book.

It is not easy to accept the reality of God as a perfect father, a father like the one Jesus described in Luke 15. Sometimes I want a father who will give me the beating I deserve. Somehow it is easier to be shamed than to be lifted out of shame. It is easier to be punished or berated than to be graciously invited to the party.

It seems like accepting the love of a perfect father should be the easiest thing in the world, and yet it is not. Like both brothers, we naturally want to pay our own way, to settle for a place in the field, and simply become a slave in the kingdom. The work of the Christian who truly wants to have intimacy with God is to accept a proper Abba theology and allow God to love us as our perfect Father.

Chapter Twenty-One

But if He is So Loving, Why...

Up to this point, we have concentrated on reprogramming our brains and hearts from believing that God is a bad or abusive Father. I have sought to help you understand that you can be "biblical," without cowering in fear. Isn't it interesting that the people who push the word "biblical" are usually trying to make us do what they want or make us afraid of our Dad? Anyway...we've been doing some undoing work. Loosening our bonds, as it were. Now the trail leads us to a darker place.

If all of this perfect father lovey-dovey stuff is true, then why are people sick and suffering and dying? Why are there meaningless wars, and why are those wars led by wicked, powerful men who destroy the weak and powerless? Why do earthquakes and hurricanes and tornadoes tear through people's lives? Why is there suffering in the world?

If we are ever to truly believe that we have a loving father, we must face the issue of suffering. Without a theology of suffering, we have no alternative but to spend our lives overlooking those things that cause confusion or bitterness, or else spend our years trying to let God off the hook, as if he needs anybody to let him off the hook.

If God needs us to let him off the hook by finding loopholes that explain how He can be good and loving and yet allow suffering, then He is not really good or loving. And we would be like an abused spouse who, in the midst of trauma bonding, constantly explains why their spouse's rage and abuse wasn't actually the abuser's fault. My relationship with my Father in heaven should not require me to play the role of the abused spouse, making apologies for Him while absorbing yet another blow.

I have started to write these next two chapters a number of times over the years. Usually, I have tried too hard to make a case for what I believe about God and suffering, writing as if I have to prove it. Those previous efforts have all fallen very short and ended up in the trash.

Suffering has been a topic of discussion and debate for as long as man has walked the earth because it has always been a central part of the human experience. I cannot address everything that has been said over thousands of years. Even if I were capable of doing so and wanted to spend the time, I would only be able to summarize the debate. I would not be able to settle it. So in this chapter, I will simply tell you my personal thoughts on the subject. I have had this conversation enough times to know that there is room for argument, so if you don't find my line of reasoning convincing, that's okay.

I went through an extended period of suffering when there was nothing I could do about it. The experience left me confused and scrambling for any foothold of hope. To make matters worse, there were times when I was able to find some hope, only to have that hope dashed. It left me in despair. I wanted to be free of hope altogether because hope ended up hurting too much.

That season of suffering also left me wondering why God would allow me to go through that pain. I could point to Bible verses that showed the good that He supposedly wanted for me and what I was supposed to do, but those verses did not square with my experience. How could He care about me and abandon me to the hurt? Here is the resolution I came to during those years, the thoughts that touched my heart and sustained me through that time of suffering and have satisfied me to this very day.

First, suffering is God's fault and it is on purpose. I know, that doesn't sound hopeful but it is to me. Not making excuses for God was critically important for me in accepting His love as my perfect Father.

Everything that has been created was created by God. I am well aware of the mental gymnastics and theological arguments that absolve God from any responsibility for sin, claiming that sin was all humanity's fault because it was Adam and Eve who ate the fruit. God didn't force them to disobey. Sin entered into the world through their actions, not God's. That's fine. It seems like a very thin argument to me, and an impractical one to boot, but it's alright if you need to keep it.

Have you heard that the Garden of Eden was perfect? Funny, the Bible never says that the Garden of Eden was perfect. It was good, yes, but not perfect. In fact, Genesis describes a number of features that were strangely imperfect. Genesis 2:15 says, "The Lord God took the man and put him in the garden of Eden to work it and keep it." Most people assume that "keep it," means to care for the animals and the vegetable gardens, to be the caretaker. However, the word in Hebrew speaks of keeping watch, guarding, to beware. Why would God set Adam as the keeper of a perfect place where there was nothing to beware of?

Glaringly, in this "perfect" garden, God chose to place a tree that would blow up all of the perfection and usher shame and suffering into the world like a Pandora's Box. If the goal of life in the garden was freedom from suffering, then I would call the inclusion of the Tree of Knowledge of Good and Evil a blatant imperfection.

And to make the situation even worse, there was a talking serpent who was hell-bent on making sure that the occupants of the garden pushed the button to launch the nuclear missile and blow the whole thing up. That is not on anyone's list of perfect places. "Hey, come to this perfect beach island. Lay out and get a tan while drinking a tasty beverage. One thing, there is a tree that will kill you and a talking animal that will try to trick you into eating it." Worse yet, God gave Adam and Eve the ability to pull the trigger and make the choice to blow the whole thing up.

The garden was delightful and beautiful. It was good. But the garden was not perfect—and it was God who made it that way. He made it that way because Adam and Eve were always supposed to eat the fruit. It wasn't as though God had one idea of how creation would work, a dream that we would always live in perfect harmony in Eden, but that plan was sabotaged by Adam and Eve when they ate the forbidden fruit, so God had to improvise. Under that scenario, redemption through Jesus was Plan B. Jesus would never have come if sin and suffering had not entered the world.

Revelation 13:7-8 says, "It (the beast) was allowed to make war on the saints and to conquer them. And authority was given it over every tribe and people and language and nation, and all who dwell on earth will worship it, everyone whose name has not been written before the foundation of the world in the book of life of the Lamb who was slain."

Fortunately, your understanding of Revelation, the version of eschatology to which you subscribe, does not matter to our point here. The Book of Revelation is full of imagery, poetry, and mysteries that are deep and powerful. However, here in chapter 13 the writer refers to a book that is mentioned a number of times in the Old Testament and many times in the New Testament: the Book of Life. In Revelation 21 the title is expanded to "the Lamb's Book of Life," but here in Revelation 13 we are given the most complete name of this book. It is called The Book of Life of the Lamb who was Slain, that was written before the foundation of the world.

Please don't get stuck on the imagery. Is it an actual book? Does the earth have foundations? The essential point is this: the book was written before creation, not as an afterthought. The book and all that it conveys were central to the purpose of creation. Creation was to accommodate the purpose of this book which was filled with the names of God's people. Also, the names in the book are tied to a lamb who would be slain. Slaughtered. Murdered. Before the foundations of the world were set, the idea of suffering was already in place, and God himself was to be the chief sufferer. Suffering was not an unfortunate byproduct of faulty design; it was the very vehicle through which God would reveal himself through the cross and draw us into a relationship with Him.

Conversations along this line are all well and good in a Bible study, whether you agree with my reasoning or not, but go to the cancer ward of a hospital and sit with a parent whose child is suffering and you'll see that this explanation is not really very helpful. There must be more. Even if we let God off the hook and say it was Adam and Eve's fault rather than His, did he not have the power to stop the suffering? God ordained and established the entire framework. He was not helpless at any point. And yet we suffer.

I am not willing to let God off the hook when He is not asking me to do it. Job, perhaps the greatest book on suffering, begins with God having a conversation with Satan and we see that permission was required before Satan could harm Job. Next, GOD GAVE PER-

MISSION for the agonizing suffering Job would go through. He gave permission for death, sickness, heartbreak, and a really horrible wife. Does that sound like God is asking to be let off the hook? That is how HE started His quintessential story about suffering.

The reason most Christians resist the suggestion that God allows suffering or that He actually set the stage for suffering to enter the world, is because they assume that it would make Him bad or evil. Is that true?

I am a father, and I sometimes cause suffering for my children for their own sake. When my young children would ask for candy before dinner, I would say no. Judging from some of the tantrums that ensued, I had evidently caused suffering. I said no to all kinds of things in ways that hurt them, angered them, and sometimes literally caused them to curse me. But I can't think of a single time I said no to them because I thought it would be fun to watch them get upset. I created or allowed for those moments of suffering for them because I saw something they didn't. They were short-sighted, I knew dinner was coming.

Of all the various sports I played while I was growing up, there was something about me and basketball coaches that just didn't mesh. I tried to quit every basketball team I was ever on midseason. Each year I would go to my father and say I wanted to quit. Each year he would tell me that I didn't have to play next year but that I had committed to that team and I would finish the season. I remember being so angry and frustrated. I was in turmoil. How could I continue to suffer through practices week after week when it would be so simple to quit?

Another time I tried to quit piano lessons, and my father told me, "You aren't good enough yet to make that decision. I'll tell you when you are good enough to quit." A few years later he came into the dining room while I was playing one of his favorite songs on the piano.

He told me it sounded wonderful and I could quit now if I wanted to. Well, I was not going to quit at that point, not after all that effort. I play piano to this day.

I do not want to trivialize the great tragedies and pain that people experience but it is important that we understand the role of suffering in the building of character. Good parents are willing to let their children suffer so that they can learn and mature and become all that they were made to be.

A long time ago I heard a man tell a story about taking his two children to the supermarket. When they arrived, they found that a petting zoo with farm animals had been set up in the parking lot. He gave each of his children a quarter and told them that he would come back to get them after he did the shopping. (This was back in the early 80s when you could leave your young children in parking lots with strangers.) He entered the store and within a few short minutes, his daughter was back at his side.

"Didn't you want to pet the animals?" he asked.

"It cost fifty cents," she said, "so I gave my quarter to my brother."

This man described several feelings that he experienced at that moment. He felt proud of his daughter for sacrificing her quarter so that her brother could gain entrance. He also immediately wanted to reach into his pocket and take out another fifty cents and give her the money so she could go enjoy the animals. But then he stopped. He thought about what would be TAKEN from her if he simply gave her fifty cents and solved the problem. He considered how it would rob her of the glory and satisfaction of the sacrifice she just made. It would buy it off, cheapen it. And at that moment he chose not to reach into his pocket.

The two of them went through the store filling their basket with what they needed, paid at the register, and then went outside and stood at the rail of the petting zoo. The two of them watched his little son, her little brother, gleefully run from animal to animal, full of joy.

I will leave it to you to decide whether or not you think the father's behavior was good or appropriate. Personally, that story always brings tears to my eyes. What a father! He was thinking about his precious daughter's character, not just her desire to pet a sheep. It's a pity there aren't more fathers in the world who care less about the petting of sheep and more about the content of their children's hearts. That kind of parenting required something. It required the father to NOT pay off his daughter's suffering. He had to let her feel it, to let her walk through the whole journey so that in the end she could feel the pride of the sacrifice she made. That experience would have been lost completely if he had given her the shortcut. The goal was to help her develop a character that could withstand harder choices than the loss of petting a stupid sheep.

Precious friends, fellow sufferers, God has the fifty cents in His pocket that could pay off all of your pain, and he chooses not to give it to you. Sometimes that breaks our hearts and sometimes we rage against him for it, but it never means that He doesn't care. It never means that He doesn't love you. I have sat with parents who are losing children to illnesses, tragedies, and wicked diseases, and I believe that they often suffer even more than their children. Oh, the pain of parents who are powerless to protect their children. Parents who can only watch helplessly as their beloved innocent children suffer. I don't think I have ever witnessed anything as heartbreaking as I've seen in those moments.

If I believe that human parents endure heartbreak when their children suffer, why is it so easy for me to take that away from God? How can I believe that my Heavenly Father is unmoved by my suffering? His decision to withhold the fifty cents is not accompanied by apathy or callousness, but by a deep pain that He shares with me in every excruciating moment.

Yes, I believe that suffering is God's fault, but I believe it is both on purpose and has a purpose, deep purpose, and that I am not left alone in my suffering because, before the foundations of the world, He had already decided that He would be the chief sufferer. He decided that He would be despised and rejected, a man of sorrows, and ultimately become sin for me on a cross where He would die.

I don't have to let God off the hook, but shame on me for leaving Him on the hook and pretending that He would feel less than I would in the face of my children's suffering. The story doesn't end here but let's let that sit for a moment. If He allowed suffering in my life AND He is my perfect Father, what must that feel like to Him? And if all of that is true, then the purpose of suffering in this life must be extraordinarily important, despite my protestations.

Chapter Twenty-Two

Packing For Eternity

If you've been to many weddings, you have doubtless heard a reading of 1 Corinthians 13. It's known as the Love Chapter. The chapter begins by listing many of the spiritual things, churchy things that we can do as Christians while pointing out that if we do not have love we gain nothing. Then the chapter defines love. Starting in verse 8, the chapter talks about all of the things that will pass away: prophecies, knowledge, tongues, and partial and incomplete gifts that will one day pass away. Pass away from what? Those things will not make it into eternity with us. They are temporary experiences that will not be important when we "shuffle off this mortal coil." Then in verse 13, we are told that three things will remain: faith, hope, and love. Remain where? The passage implies that those three will continue INTO our eternal experience after death.

That is a monumentally huge statement. One category of things will pass away when we die. They will no longer matter. Only three things will remain with us. Let's unpack this carefully.

When I was a child, I did not look forward to heaven. Don't get me wrong, I didn't want hell, so getting to heaven was my obvious choice, but I wasn't looking forward to it. I was told I would live in some celestial city. I had my pictorial Pilgrim's Progress comic book, so I knew what it looked like. Its streets were paved with gold, I would spend my entire day worshiping God, and I would cast the crown that I had earned during my time on earth at His feet. Those were the main features of THE REST OF ETERNITY as they were described to me at my Christian school.

People, we've got to do better talking to kids!

First of all, think about worshiping God all day. When I was a third-grader, it sounded like I would be expected to go to choir all day, every day. That didn't sound good. I only had to go to my school's choir class once a week and participate on special occasions at church, and in neither case did I enjoy it. So that's what was waiting for me in heaven, to spend every day, all day, in choir? That would be marginally better than hell, admittedly, but only marginally.

And what about those streets paved with gold? I grew up on the Salinas river in California. The river was my playground, the place I wanted to be. I didn't want to be trapped in some gaudy urban sprawl. Give me some pine trees! Gold streets would be better than hell, I guess, but was there a choice with some trees?

And what about throwing my crown at Jesus's feet? Would the affirmation and congratulation I received for a life well lived, "Well done, good and faithful servant," be immediately dismissed, and the reward returned? That didn't seem right. Not to mention that Scripture says it was the elders who did that casting, not all of the people, but whatever, don't let the Bible get in the way of our favorite misconceptions. It's not like He is unworthy of all of our crowns, but still...not what the Bible actually says.

My point, beyond the fact that many of those images and ideas of "heaven" that were given to me as a child were unbiblical or strangely skewed, is that the descriptions of eternity that I was handed were not terribly appealing. Heaven was simply a better option than hell. In

1 Corinthians 13, by contrast, we get a glimpse of an eternity that is amazing.

Three things remain. Although they belong to our eternal existence and experience, two of them make no sense at all. Love is eternal, of course. That's easy. God is love, so of course, love will be central to whatever infinite life will be like. But faith? Hope?

My favorite definition of faith is this: trusting in God's provision to receive His promises. Great. What exactly will I need faith for in eternity, when I will "know as I am known?" When I was a child, I was taught that after I die I am going to understand everything. I will know God. That prospect is appealing on some levels and incredibly distasteful on others. The greatest adventures in my life have been faith adventures. The greatest thrills come when I lept without knowing what is on the other side.

What will faith look like in eternity? Hell if I know. What I do know is that faith WILL BE a part of my eternal experience. It will be a part of my existence. I will know faith in the context of knowledge and trust, faith at a level higher than anything I have ever experienced here. That will be amazing! The adventure will not end when I die, because faith will abide.

Hope is even weirder to consider. As far as I can imagine from where I am today, all of my hopes will be consummated in eternity. My hopes will be fulfilled. Why in the world would I still need or have hope in eternity? We all know, and studies have proven, that anticipation contributes more to my joy than acquisition. That's the fun of Christmas for children, the hope and longing. Many of the toys that are unwrapped on Christmas morning will be set aside and barely touched within days, but oh the mouth-watering anticipation of what might be inside that brightly wrapped box! Hope is beautiful, powerful, and full of surprises.

Hope also changes and grows as I grow. I can clearly remember my dearest hope during my preschool years. There were two pedal cars with steering wheels in the play area. Every day, as recess approached, I would inch toward the door, hoping that I would be able to ride in a vehicle with a steering wheel. Don't judge me. I was four. That was my hope. At six years old I wanted a particular kind of shoes, the ones with a zipper and a small pocket in the side that could hold two pennies if you were lucky. I think they were called Kangaroos or something like that. How I burned with desire and hope for those shoes! In junior high, I hoped for a locker of my very own, a private place where I could safely store my organizer and protect it with a lock whose combination was known only to me.

None of those earlier versions of me could have anticipated the contemporary hopes of this divorced 45-year-old who is riding a stationary bike and typing in the early hours of the morning. The 25-year-old version of me would not have imagined that many of his hopes would eventually be laid aside because they did not serve me well. And the me I am today cannot imagine what hope will look like when I enter into my final years and the closing moments of my life. Deep hope is progressive, and always connected to my experience and wisdom. It can certainly be regressive and attached to foolishness, but it always moves with what I know and experience.

With that in mind, can you imagine what hope will look like on the other side of eternity? The very thought that I will still have things to hope for is wonderful. Even more amazing is the thought that my hope in those days will come in light of my new knowledge and insight into real and deep spiritual things, into the person of God. Sign me up for that journey — I'm in!

The promise that faith, hope, and love will endure makes me long for eternity in my Daddy's kingdom. Those three things make this life full of suffering worth living, and I can't wait to experience all three untainted by my own foolishness and confusion.

But that is eternity, some time off in the future. What about now? According to I Corinthians 13, these three things remain, which means that they are here right now and will be afterward. I deeply resent the notion that eternal life starts after we die. What a silly thought. We are alive right now and we believe that we will continue to live after we die. Ergo, obviously, this is all my life. Now and then. I'm in eternal life right now, it will just change when I die.

Imagine your life plotted on a yardstick. If you are in the midst of suffering and every day is dragging on like a ball and chain, your life probably feels very long. But remember, you don't stop living when you die. You just stop living here. You will not cease to be you. You will go on. So in the context of eternity, how long is your time here on this spinning orb, full of longing and suffering? How would you mark it on the three-foot stick if that stick represented eternity?

I expect to be around here for 70 or 80 years. In light of eternity, that number hardly registers. My time on earth is by far the smallest piece of my experience of being me. It only seems long because I have only known life and death within this time frame. Your current state of life is a blip. It is so short. And that is not a depressing thought, that is a gracious thought.

What makes this tiny speck of time so unique? Another evangelical saying that I hope I never have to hear again is, "The only thing you can do here on earth that you can't do in heaven is lead someone to Christ." Really? How about having a horribly shitty year? Isn't that something I can do here that I can't do in heaven? How about sitting in the ashes of my life and doubting that God has an ounce of concern for my feelings or heart? And that, my friend, is the point.

Suffering is one of your experiences that is unique to this tiny bit of time. Suffering. That feeling that drives me deeper into faith, desperate faith. Suffering. The experience that makes me cling to hope. Suffering. That pain that requires me to forgive, to be forgiven, and to cling to love for comfort.

These three things remain. Only these three. These are the three things I can pack into my eternal luggage and unpack on the other side of the grave. Only these three beautiful experiences and all of them are aided, deepened, and refined by...suffering. NEVER in all the rest of my existence will I know faith, hope, or love as I can see them through the lens of this kind of suffering. Only during this brief instant, this particle of time.

Only now can I know hope through death and grief. Only now can I know faith through this level of blindness. And still, I often hear myself and others pray for God to remove suffering. Hey, even Jesus prayed that the cup of suffering would pass. That's a very human request. But Jesus completed the circle in his prayer and in the end submitted to the Father's design for that small season of His eternal existence. The Father said no to the removal of the cup and Jesus went to the cross.

Friends, if I'm going to have to endure the suffering that is caused by my stupid decisions, the stupid decisions of others, and the general chaos of a broken world, I really don't want to waste the experience. I know I can't avoid it, so I want to order the biggest matched luggage set I can find and in the midst of suffering ask myself, "What is there to hope for in this? What is there to believe? What does love look like in the ashes?" I may not be able to answer those questions perfectly in my pain, nor is it likely that I will be able to summon the strength to climb out of the pit, but that is where I will start. God, keep me from wasting the pain. Keep me from squandering this speck of time.

I am here in this experience where God ordained and allowed suffering. It is an insanely short period of time and I don't want to spend it avoiding the most unique feature of it. He didn't give me the opportunity because of a lack of love and He didn't make it longer than it ought to be.

These three remain. One of my great hopes for eternity is that I will get to invite Dietrich Bonhoeffer over for a meal and tell him to bring his faith, hope, and love souvenirs. As we sit and eat, he will show me those things that remain and talk about them. I will listen, ask questions, and marvel at what matters. I will be in awe of all the ways that our Father was a perfect father—even in the midst of World War II. Dietrick and I will see it, and that will be worship.

Can I trust God during this speck of time? Can I believe that there is a purpose bigger than I can see? I do not have a lot of core convictions that I insist on, I'm always growing and changing, and sometimes I shrink as well, but this I believe from the bottom of my heart. When I die and my vision finally expands, I will be satisfied by the answers I receive. I don't have the answers now, and I don't know what form they will take then, but I believe I will be satisfied.

If I had all of the answers now, suffering would be of almost no use. Suffering happens mostly in the mind and not in the thing itself. During this brief breath of time, I am, at my best, ignorant and blind. All of life on this planet is lived by faith, whether you believe in God or not. It is hope deferred and confusion in faith that causes our mental suffering. For me, experiencing God in the darkness and discovering the gift of faith REQUIRES the darkness. And in the end, I will be satisfied.

At the beginning of our conversation about suffering I talked about various ways that the Garden of Eden was not perfect. Here is its biggest deliberate flaw. Man and woman knew God in the garden and had the opportunity to walk with Him in the cool of the evening. When sin entered into the world, they declined the invitation and hid instead.

Today, I can know Him even better than they did. Through the person and work of Jesus and His indwelling Spirit, I can walk with Him despite my sins. I can grope and grapple for His love and indeed can find it in the middle of suffering and in a sea of tears. And for this short period of time, He suffers with me and holds me in His perfect love. They didn't have that in the garden. They didn't have adoption paid for by the lamb that was slain. I believe that my life is better.

Chapter Twenty-Three

What Now?

So now what? What do I do with this information about my Perfect Father? Where do I even begin?

First, in each moment where you feel guilt, shame, or judgment, start asking this question, "Dad...what do you think about me?"

Remember, you are answering this question in your own mind, so use your Perfect Father sheet and the corrective information we have covered in this little book. A Pharisee answering that question would probably have God cosign his legalism. We won't do that. Because we believe that Jesus did enough to bring us into a perfect relationship with a perfect Father, we will take our shame and pain straight to the Father and find comfort in His love, grace, and admonition.

When I ask that question of my heavenly Father I don't expect that He will simply say that everything is okay. There may be consequences. There may be discipline, but there will always be love. My father will never quit on me. He will never turn me away. "I will never leave you, I will never forsake you."

Likewise, whenever you hear someone—whether a friend or a pastor— talking about God, ask yourself the question, "Does this description of God show him to be a perfect Father, or something else? Is there truly no condemnation in Christ that is being handed to me right now, or is it Jesus plus something else to win God's love?"

I apologize in advance for the hard path that will result from asking that question. You are probably going to find that people you love are pushing a version of God that, if the same standard was applied to an earthly father, would be considered abusive or neglectful father. On the other hand, you may hear God described as a Father who is never disappointed and who treats sin and inappropriate behavior as if it didn't matter. In those moments you will have to decide what to do. You will have to decide how to exhibit the very grace and compassion that I hope you have found in the journey we have taken together in this book.

The first tool is simple. Don't deviate from your Abba theology. Don't be intimidated into abandoning your understanding of who God is TOWARD you because of the person and work of Jesus.

The second tool comes from a Bible verse that I learned as a child and still treasure today. Proverbs 3:5-6 tells us, "Trust in the Lord with all your heart, lean not on your own understanding, in all your ways acknowledge Him and He will direct your paths."

That is one of the most practical verses in all of scripture. It contains one principle, two practicals, and one promise all bundled together in a neat package. The first call is to trust in the Lord with all of your heart. That should invoke lots of Christiany feelings, along with the recognition that, although I would love to trust the Lord with all my heart, I really don't have the first clue about how to practically do that.

That's not a problem. We are simply told to live by that principle and then we will find our paths directed, or have them made straight. Trust in the Lord with all our hearts. The practicals are sandwiched between the principle and the promise, between trusting and having our paths made straight.

The first practical instruction is this, do not lean on what you think you know. Don't put any weight on the first thoughts that come to your mind. This is easy to say but hard to do, learning to pause before we act on our knowledge and experience.

Let's be clear. We know a lot of good things, and this verse is not telling us that those things are not good or correct. We can draw on prior experience in order to make sound decisions in similar situations. That is not bad. This verse is simply telling us to stop, to pause what might otherwise be an instant and automatic response. Don't assume that yesterday's insight is fit for today's struggle. It may be, but there may be something new to learn. There may be some new way to respond.

It is tragic how quickly we can allow knowledge to replace the Holy Spirit. We only need the Spirit to guide us into one truth and then we can take it from there. We can fall into the trap of extrapolating from prior experiences. If I deal with Joe today based on how I dealt with Allen eight years ago in a situation that seems very similar I can avoid a whole lot of prayer and listening by simply applying Allen's solution to Joe. The temptation to do so makes it hard for us to not lean on our own understanding. We must honor the things we know and the wisdom we have gained from experience, while at the same time not leaving God out of the process today.

The second practical step in trusting the Lord with all our hearts will make pausing a little easier. Having first been told NOT to do something, we are now given something to focus on instead, of something TO DO. After we have paused and not put weight on what we think we know, we are instructed to acknowledge Him in all our ways. That's step two. Acknowledge Him.

Funny how we can make such a simple and practical piece of instruction churchy. How does one acknowledge God? By prayer? Okay, sure. But what kind of prayer? Most of my prayers are telling God how

I want things to go; there is very little listening in my moment-to-moment prayers.

Let's take God out of the equation for a moment. Let's picture me walking into a room and my friend John is sitting in the corner. How do I acknowledge Him? Simple. I acknowledge him by saying, "Hey, John." I see him, I know he is in the room, I acknowledge the fact that I see him and he is in the room. It's not rocket surgery.

But see what happens when I stop throughout my day to say, "Hey, Dad." That simple practice helps me remember that God actually exists, that he hears me, that he is with me, and that I am not alone at any moment. It's that simple. I stop and acknowledge Him just as I would any other person in the room.

Now, if John was in the room when I got a hard phone call, I could acknowledge him by telling him how annoying and hard the phone call was. I could share what was happening in me at that moment. Sometimes that is how prayers look at their best. If God is my Father and He is interested in the small things, then He is interested in how each moment feels. I don't have to make it any more complicated or churchy than that.

If I were talking to my earthly father, I would not initiate a conversation about that hard phone call by saying, "Oh father that brought me forth from thine loins, I beseech thee to listen to my grievance about a crappy phone call that I have just now received." I would probably simply say, "Man, I just got a call from an idiot. I'm so frustrated." He would then listen as I explained why the person on the phone was an idiot.

That's how we are invited to be talking to Abba. We don't need to clean up our language for His delicate ears. If you're not convinced on this point, read the Psalms. David railed AT God sometimes. He made unfiltered complaints about his trials, his enemies, his terrors, and his resentment about the absence of justice in this world. Let's take permission from the Holy Scriptures and start being honest with our Father in our daily prayers.

There is one more layer to acknowledging God. If I only acknowledge people by speaking to them, I am not in a relationship with them. If I complain to John about the crappy phone call but never want to hear his thoughts on it, then I have made him my vomitorium. He is just a person that I like to throw up on because I know he will take it and listen with a compassionate ear. If I am in a relationship with John, however, I will listen as he either comforts me or tells me that maybe I was the idiot on the phone call.

To acknowledge God begins with acknowledging his presence, but it also includes accepting that He, as my Father and as God, has an opinion about me and every situation I am in. This is where acknowledging Him, "in all your ways," becomes life-changing.

I am prone to only acknowledge God for the big things. Acknowledging Him in all my ways seems like I'm wasting both of our time for some reason. However, that's not how I look at conversations with my children. My daughter just started her first job, and every day when she comes home I ask her about it. I ask about the people she worked with and how she liked them, even though I had never met any of them. She tells me about customers in the restaurant who were rude or who were kind, customers who glared, and customers who smiled. And I love hearing every single detail. If I, clothed in flesh and far from perfect, feel that way about the mundane details of my daughter's work day, how much more does my Father in heaven?

Here's another example. At this point in my life, I do a fairly uneventful job. I sit in front of a computer all day. Where in that boring routine is it appropriate for me to acknowledge God? Why would I bug God with such silly and small things as, "Hey Dad, sitting here in front of the computer for the millionth hour, I'm feeling pretty unmotivated." Why would God want to hear that? Answer: because He's my father and he cares about even the mundane parts of my life.

So in acknowledging God during my work day, I can pause and say, "Hey Dad, how's it going (remember and acknowledge that He is there)? Do you have any thoughts about my day?" And then I sit and think about that. I don't know exactly what God's thoughts are at any given moment, but what I do have is my own perfect father worksheet, which describes a little bit about the Heavenly Father I believe in.

So how would a perfect father feel about his kid putting in a hard day's work to earn money to pay for food and shelter for his family? How would a perfect father feel about those long days when life feels boring and tedious? It's not hard to answer that. I know how I would feel, and I'm not a perfect father. I would respond to any of my children by saying, "I am so proud of you. I know this is not the most exciting thing for you to be doing, but you are hanging in there, and I love that about you. You are pushing through and not quitting. Good job! keep it up! You are such a delight to watch, and you are such a good dad in how you are taking care of the family I entrusted you with."

After considering what a perfect father would say, I acknowledge God again. I acknowledge that He is aware, so deeply aware of my moment and my feelings. I acknowledge that he is my perfect Father and that because of Jesus I am perfectly delightful to him in all of my moments. I let the love that I know must be at the center of His heart wash over me.

That is what acknowledging God looks like at those times when I remember to do it, and every time I do I get the sensation that I just got a big hug from my Daddy. That feeling allows me to face my work with a different attitude because He has given it its proper place and purpose in my life. He has reminded me that I don't have to be doing "ministry" work for work to be a ministry or to have a profound purpose. He infuses even my simplest duties with honor.

I follow the same process when I am struggling with shame or doubt, or when I am blindsided by unexpected events. I take out my Perfect Father sheet and ask my Abba, "How do you feel about this? What do you see? Who am I?" And every time the answer comes from a Father who graciously keeps inviting me back home for a party. It comes from a Father who wants to make an omelet with me without fear that I will mess it up. It comes from someone whose perfect love casts out all my fears. Even in my brokenness, I can approach Him boldly and climb up on his lap for a snuggle.

After I have acknowledged Him and tasted His grace and love again, my direction is clear and straight. My heart is calm. And if I'm confused again 15 minutes later, I can do it all over again. He has never rolled His eyes at my return visits, and I am certain that He will not roll His eyes at you. He is El Shaddai. As often as I have taken sustenance from Him, He is sufficient to let me feed again at the wellspring of grace.

Once we learn to do this in our day-to-day moments, the really unimportant ones, then we can do it within our relationships. If you want to mess up any joy of being right in an argument, acknowledge God. Literally, pause when things are winding up, ask for a moment, then tell God what you are feeling and if He has any thoughts on the conversation that is going down. I promise you it will be painful in that moment but the end results will be far better than you could have achieved on your own.

The Gospel was not meant to be academic. It is transformative, which means it is supposed to change us. Not just our behavior, the Gospel changes the lens through which we see all of life. In that way, it changes how we feel. A version of Christianity that does not cause any change in perception or emotion is a waste of time—at least it is for me at this point in my life. I've already put in my time doing Churchianity. It wasn't all bad, and it wasn't all good, but at this point, I just want to experience what it really means to be a Christian. I don't need to look more Christian. I want to discover the face and heart of my Daddy every day.

My friend, I hope you discover that face and heart too, for I know that once you have seen it you will never be able to unsee it, and that seeing it will change you forever.

Made in the USA
Columbia, SC
13 October 2024

43537411R00104